Parenting Kids with PTSD

Essential Strategies and Support for Nurturing Your Child Through Trauma

CLARA JENNINGS

Table of Contents

Introduction

Imagine waking up every day to the sound of your child's fearful cries. That was my reality when my daughter, Lily, was 7 years old. One night, a loud thunderstorm hit, and the lightning struck very close to our home. The fear from that night left a lasting imprint on Lily. She began to react to the slightest noise or change in routine with intense anxiety. Everyday activities that once seemed normal became sources of stress for her. I felt overwhelmed, unsure of how to help Lily or how to provide the comfort and security she desperately needed.

PTSD, or Post-Traumatic Stress Disorder, is a serious condition that can develop after a child experiences or witnesses something deeply upsetting or frightening. For Lily, it was the storm that shattered her sense of safety. She began to experience nightmares, had frequent flashbacks, and became incredibly jumpy. The world outside seemed like a dangerous place to her, and her sense of security was shattered. As a parent, watching my child suffer and feeling powerless to change her pain was heart-wrenching.

Understanding PTSD was my first step toward helping Lily navigate this challenging time. It became clear that PTSD affects more than just a child's mind; it impacts their emotions, behaviors, and physical health. Lily's fears were not just about the storm but about every loud noise and sudden change in her environment. Her daily routines became overwhelming, and her relationships with family and friends suffered as she withdrew into herself.

Parenting a child with PTSD requires patience, empathy, and a willingness to learn and adapt. This book is designed to provide you with essential strategies and support to nurture your child through trauma. You might find yourself questioning your ability to cope or wondering if you're doing enough. These feelings are natural, but it's important to remember that you are not alone. Many parents have walked this path and have found ways to support their children effectively.

In this book, we will explore practical approaches to creating a safe and supportive environment at home. This includes establishing routines that help your child feel secure and using communication strategies that foster openness and trust. You'll learn how to recognize the signs of PTSD and understand the importance of working with professionals who can offer specialized help. Self-care for you as a parent is also crucial, as managing your own well-being directly impacts your ability to support your child.

Each chapter will delve into the unique challenges of parenting a child with PTSD and provide actionable steps to address these challenges. We'll look at how to support your child's emotional regulation, tackle everyday problems with effective strategies, and foster resilience and hope. Additionally, we'll guide you in finding and utilizing resources and support networks that can further aid you and your family.

By understanding PTSD and implementing these strategies, you can help your child build resilience and find hope amidst their struggles. Your role is vital, and this book aims to equip you with the knowledge and tools needed to make a significant difference in your child's life. Together, we can navigate this journey with compassion and strength, just as I did with Lily.

Chapter 1
Understanding PTSD in Children

When we talk about PTSD, or Post-Traumatic Stress Disorder, we're referring to a serious mental health condition that can develop after a child has experienced or witnessed something very disturbing or frightening. For children, this might be anything from a car accident or a natural disaster to experiencing or witnessing abuse or violence. PTSD can affect how a child thinks, feels, and behaves, making everyday life very challenging for them.

For many kids, the world suddenly feels unsafe after a traumatic event. They may become overly anxious, easily startled, or withdrawn. The trauma doesn't just go away on its own; it lingers, making the child feel like they're always on guard. It's like their body and mind are in a constant state of alert, always preparing for something bad to happen.

Children with PTSD may experience a range of symptoms. They might have frequent nightmares or flashbacks that make them relive the traumatic event. These can be very distressing and can interfere with their ability to sleep or focus on daily activities. Kids may also avoid situations that remind them of the trauma, which can limit their social interactions and participation in activities they used to enjoy. This avoidance can make them feel isolated and disconnected from others.

PTSD can also affect a child's behavior. They might become more aggressive, irritable, or have difficulty controlling their emotions. Some children might regress to behaviors they had outgrown, like bed-wetting or clinging to parents. These reactions are often confusing and frustrating for parents who might not understand why their child is acting this way.

Understanding PTSD in children involves recognizing these symptoms and knowing that they are not just about being difficult or misbehaving. The child's reactions are a way of coping with overwhelming emotions and memories. It's important to remember that PTSD is not the child's fault; it's a response to an event that was beyond their control.

Supporting a child with PTSD means providing a stable, safe environment where they can begin to heal. This involves offering reassurance and understanding, maintaining consistent routines, and encouraging open communication about their feelings. It's also crucial to be patient and give your child time to process their experiences. They need to know that they are safe and loved, and that it's okay to talk about their fears and concerns.

By learning about PTSD and its effects, you can better understand what your child is going through and how to support them. This knowledge will help you create a nurturing environment where your child can start to feel more secure and begin to heal from their traumatic experiences.

Symptoms and behaviors associated with PTSD in different age groups

Children with PTSD exhibit a range of symptoms and behaviors that can vary based on their age. Understanding these differences can help you better support your child through their recovery. Here's a breakdown of how PTSD symptoms might appear across different age groups:

Preschoolers (Ages 3-5)
For very young children, PTSD can manifest in ways that might seem confusing or unexpected. They might have nightmares or fear the dark. Behavioral changes such as increased clinginess, difficulty sleeping, or regression to earlier behaviors like thumb-sucking or bed-wetting can be signs of PTSD. Preschoolers might not have the words to express their feelings, so they may act out their fears through play or exhibit sudden bursts of anger or frustration. They might also avoid situations or places that remind them of the trauma, even if they cannot articulate why.

Early Elementary Age (Ages 6-8)
Children in this age group might start to show more specific signs of PTSD. They may experience frequent flashbacks or intrusive thoughts about the traumatic event. Nightmares might become more common, and they may struggle with separation anxiety, finding it hard to be away from their parents or caregivers. School performance might suffer due to trouble concentrating, and they might withdraw from friends or

activities they once enjoyed. Emotional outbursts, such as tantrums or aggressive behavior, can also be indicative of their distress.

Late Elementary and Early Middle School (Ages 9-12)

As children get older, their symptoms can become more apparent and varied. They might start to have more pronounced symptoms of anxiety, such as excessive worry, physical complaints like stomachaches or headaches, or frequent avoidance of reminders of the trauma. They may also experience mood swings, irritability, or trouble in school, such as difficulties with concentration and academic performance. Older children might have difficulty trusting others or forming relationships, which can lead to social isolation. They might also engage in risky behaviors or act out as a way of coping with their feelings.

Teenagers (Ages 13-18)

Teenagers with PTSD often show symptoms similar to adults, though they might still express their distress differently. They might experience intense flashbacks, nightmares, or severe anxiety. Mood swings, irritability, and depression can be more pronounced, and they might turn to substance abuse or self-harm as a way to cope with their pain. Teens might also struggle with relationships and social interactions, finding it hard to trust others or maintain friendships. Changes in behavior, such as increased secrecy or withdrawal from family, can be signs that they are struggling with PTSD.

Understanding how PTSD manifests in different age groups can help you recognize the signs in your child and tailor your approach to their needs. It's important to approach each child with empathy and patience, offering support and stability as they work through their trauma. By being aware of these symptoms and behaviors, you can better assist your child in navigating their healing journey.

Common Triggers and Their Impact on Children

Triggers are specific situations, events, or stimuli that can cause a child with PTSD to relive their traumatic experience or experience heightened anxiety and distress. Understanding these triggers is crucial for helping your child navigate their daily life and manage their PTSD. Here's a look at common triggers and how they can impact children:

1. Sensory Triggers

Children with PTSD might be especially sensitive to sensory inputs such as loud noises, bright lights, or certain smells. For example, the sound of a thunderstorm might remind a child of a traumatic event related to a storm. Similarly, certain smells or sounds can trigger memories or feelings associated with their trauma, causing them to feel scared or anxious. These sensory triggers can make everyday environments feel overwhelming and unsafe.

2. Situational Triggers

Certain situations or places that remind a child of their traumatic experience can act as triggers. For instance, if a child was in a car accident, they might feel anxious or scared when they are in a car or see a car crash on television. School environments, specific locations, or even routine activities can become sources of stress if they remind the child of their trauma. This can lead to avoidance behavior, where the child might refuse to go to certain places or participate in activities they once enjoyed.

3. Emotional Triggers

Emotional triggers are situations or interactions that provoke strong feelings related to the trauma. For example, a child who experienced loss might feel overwhelmed by grief during events like anniversaries or family gatherings. Emotional triggers can cause a child to become more withdrawn, irritable, or upset. They might struggle with their emotions, leading to outbursts or increased anxiety.

4. Interpersonal Triggers

Interactions with others can also be a trigger for children with PTSD. If a child has experienced abuse or trauma related to relationships, they might react strongly to conflicts or confrontations with peers or family members. They may struggle with trust and have difficulty forming or maintaining friendships. Situations that involve conflict or criticism can heighten their feelings of fear or insecurity.

5. Media and External Stimuli

Exposure to media that depicts violence, accidents, or other distressing events can be a significant trigger for children with PTSD. News stories, movies, or even video games that include traumatic content can provoke flashbacks or increase anxiety. It's important to monitor the media your child consumes and discuss their reactions to ensure they feel safe and supported.

Impact of Triggers

Triggers can have a profound impact on a child's behavior and emotional well-being. When triggered, a child might experience intense fear or panic, leading to physical symptoms such as a racing heart or sweating. Their reactions can include crying, screaming, or withdrawing from others. They might also exhibit increased aggression or become more isolated.

Understanding and managing triggers involves creating a supportive environment where your child feels safe and secure. It can help to identify potential triggers and develop strategies to address them. For example, helping your child practice relaxation techniques or grounding exercises can assist them in managing their reactions. Open communication about their triggers and providing reassurance can also make a significant difference in their ability to cope with their PTSD.

By recognizing and addressing triggers, you can help your child navigate their feelings and experiences more effectively, supporting their journey toward healing and resilience.

Explanation of Trauma Responses and Coping Mechanisms

When a child experiences trauma, their response can vary widely, influenced by their age, personality, and the nature of the trauma. Understanding these responses and how children cope with them is essential in providing effective support.

Trauma responses are often intense and can manifest in various ways. One common response is hypervigilance. This means that the child is constantly on edge, as if they are always expecting something bad to happen. They might be easily startled, have trouble relaxing, or appear overly alert. This state of heightened awareness is the body's way of staying prepared for perceived threats but can be exhausting and overwhelming for the child.

Another response is dissociation, where the child feels disconnected from their surroundings or even from themselves. They might seem spaced out or detached, as if they are watching events from a distance rather than fully participating. This can be a coping mechanism that helps them manage overwhelming emotions but can make it difficult for them to engage with others and their environment.

Children might also experience flashbacks or intrusive thoughts. Flashbacks make them feel like they are reliving the traumatic event, which can be terrifying and disorienting. Intrusive thoughts can be persistent and distressing, making it hard for them to focus on anything else. Both responses can interfere with their daily functioning and overall well-being.

Coping mechanisms are the strategies children use to manage the emotional and psychological impact of trauma. These mechanisms can be both healthy and unhealthy. Healthy coping strategies include seeking comfort from trusted adults, engaging in creative activities like drawing or writing, and using relaxation techniques such as deep breathing or mindfulness exercises. These strategies help children process their feelings and reduce anxiety.

Unhealthy coping mechanisms might include avoidance, where the child avoids places, people, or activities that remind them of the trauma. They might also engage in risky behaviors or self-harm as a way to express or numb their emotional pain. It's important to recognize these unhealthy patterns and seek professional help if necessary.

As a parent, understanding your child's trauma responses and coping mechanisms can help you provide appropriate support. Encouraging open communication, creating a stable and reassuring environment, and modeling healthy coping strategies can make a significant difference. It's also important to be patient and recognize that healing from trauma is a gradual process.

By being attuned to your child's responses and supporting them with effective coping strategies, you can help them navigate their emotions and experiences more effectively, fostering resilience and hope for their future.

Chapter 2
Key signs and symptoms of PTSD in children

Understanding PTSD in children involves knowing the key signs and symptoms that indicate a child might be struggling with this condition. Recognizing these signs early can make a big difference in how quickly and effectively your child gets the help they need. Here's a detailed look at the key signs and symptoms of PTSD in children:

1. Emotional Distress
Children with PTSD often experience intense emotional distress. They may have frequent mood swings or sudden outbursts of anger, sadness, or frustration. This emotional turmoil can seem unpredictable, with the child reacting strongly to things that might not bother other children. They might also appear numb or detached at times, struggling to express their feelings in a typical way.

2. Recurrent Memories
A common sign of PTSD is the repeated re-experiencing of the traumatic event. This can show up as intrusive thoughts or flashbacks, where the child feels as though they are reliving the traumatic experience. They might talk about the event often or seem preoccupied with it. Nightmares related to the trauma are also common, causing significant distress and sleep disturbances.

3. Avoidance Behavior

Children with PTSD might go out of their way to avoid anything that reminds them of the trauma. This can include avoiding certain places, people, or activities. For example, if a child witnessed a car accident, they might refuse to get into a car or avoid areas where the accident happened. This avoidance can interfere with their daily routines and social interactions.

4. Hypervigilance

Hypervigilance is a state of heightened alertness where the child is overly aware of their surroundings, often feeling like danger is always imminent. They might startle easily, be overly anxious, or have difficulty relaxing. This constant state of alert can make it hard for them to focus on everyday tasks and interact with others comfortably.

5. Behavioral Changes

PTSD can lead to noticeable changes in a child's behavior. They might become more aggressive or act out in ways they didn't before. Some children might regress to earlier behaviors, such as thumb-sucking or bed-wetting. These changes can be confusing for parents but are often a way for the child to cope with their distress.

6. Social Withdrawal

Children with PTSD might withdraw from social activities and relationships. They may isolate themselves from friends and family, preferring to be alone. This withdrawal can be a way to avoid situations that remind them of the trauma or because they feel disconnected from others. They might also struggle to form or maintain friendships, finding it hard to trust people.

7. Difficulty Concentrating

PTSD can affect a child's ability to concentrate and focus on tasks. They might have trouble paying attention at school, leading to poor academic performance or difficulty completing assignments. This lack of focus can be due to their preoccupation with the traumatic event or from the emotional distress they are experiencing.

8. Physical Symptoms

Sometimes, PTSD manifests through physical symptoms such as headaches, stomachaches, or other unexplained aches and pains. These physical complaints can be a way for the child to express their emotional pain or distress, especially if they find it hard to articulate their feelings verbally.

Recognizing these signs and symptoms in your child is the first step towards getting them the help they need. It's crucial to handle the situation with empathy and awareness. If you notice several of these signs, it's a good idea to consult with a mental health professional who can provide a proper diagnosis and recommend appropriate treatment.

By being attentive to these key signs of PTSD, you can better support your child and ensure they receive the care and assistance they need to manage their trauma and start their journey towards healing.

Behavioral and emotional indicators

As a mother, watching my child struggle can be heart-wrenching. I remember the days when my daughter, who we'll call Lily, seemed to change before my eyes. It was as if a cloud had settled over her once-bright personality. These changes were not just in the way she acted but also in the way she felt and expressed her emotions. Recognizing these behavioral and emotional indicators was a crucial step in understanding what Lily was going through.

In the early days, I noticed that Lily's behavior became erratic. She would go from being cheerful to suddenly angry or upset, often without any clear reason. It was confusing and, at times, overwhelming to witness. Her outbursts were intense, and it felt as if the smallest things could set her off. Simple requests, like finishing her homework or picking up her toys, would sometimes result in tears or a tantrum. I knew this wasn't just typical child behavior; it was something deeper, something more troubling.

Emotionally, Lily seemed to retreat into herself. She became quiet, her laughter less frequent, and her once lively conversations turned into brief, hesitant responses. I could see that she was struggling to express what she was feeling. It was as if there was a wall between her and the world, and no matter how hard she tried, she couldn't seem to break through it. Her withdrawal was not just from me but from her friends and activities she once loved. It was heartbreaking to see her isolate herself, a stark contrast to the vibrant child she used to be.

Her ability to concentrate also began to wane. Tasks that were once easy for her, like reading a book or finishing a drawing, now seemed like monumental challenges. It was painful to watch her struggle with focus, as if her mind was clouded by something she couldn't quite understand or articulate. Her teachers at school also mentioned that she seemed distracted and less engaged in class, a sign that her emotional state was affecting her ability to function normally.

The physical symptoms were another area of concern. Lily began complaining of frequent headaches and stomachaches, which seemed to have no clear medical cause. These physical complaints were not just a reflection of her emotional distress but also a manifestation of the anxiety and fear she was experiencing. It was difficult to see her in discomfort and not be able to immediately alleviate her pain.

As a parent, recognizing these behavioral and emotional indicators was the first step in seeking help. It required me to be observant and empathetic, understanding that Lily's reactions were not just random or attention-seeking but were deeply tied to her inner turmoil. I realized that her behaviors were not just symptoms but cries for help, signals that she needed support and understanding.

Understanding these indicators allowed me to approach Lily with more compassion and patience. It meant providing her with a safe space to express her emotions and seeking professional help to address her needs. This journey was not easy, but it was essential in helping Lily navigate through her trauma and begin the path toward healing. Recognizing and responding to these signs is crucial for any parent dealing with a child who has PTSD, as it sets the foundation for effective support and intervention.

Behavioral Indicators

As a parent, being attuned to the behavioral and emotional indicators of PTSD is crucial for understanding and supporting your child. When my daughter, whom we'll refer to as Lily, started showing signs of distress, it became evident that her behavior and emotions were deeply intertwined with her trauma. Observing these indicators closely helped me to better address her needs and provide the support she required.

One significant behavioral change to watch for is an increase in aggression or irritability. Children with PTSD may have difficulty managing their emotions, leading to outbursts of anger or frustration that seem disproportionate to the situation. For instance, Lily would sometimes react harshly to minor issues, such as a disagreement with a sibling or a slight change in routine. This aggression was often a result of her heightened state of anxiety and an inability to cope with her overwhelming feelings.

Another behavioral indicator is a noticeable decline in daily functioning. This might manifest as a drop in academic performance, neglect of personal hygiene, or a lack of interest in previously enjoyed activities. Lily's schoolwork suffered as she struggled to concentrate and complete assignments. She also became disinterested in activities she once loved, like drawing and playing with friends. This withdrawal from daily activities can be a sign that the child is overwhelmed and struggling to cope with their emotions.

Emotional Indicators

Emotional indicators are just as important to recognize. A child with PTSD may experience pervasive feelings of fear or sadness. They might appear unusually anxious or have frequent episodes of crying for no apparent reason. Lily often seemed fearful, even in safe and familiar environments. She would startle easily at loud noises or sudden movements, reflecting her heightened state of alertness and fear.

It's also important to watch for signs of dissociation. Children with PTSD might appear detached from reality, as if they are not fully present. They might have difficulty focusing on conversations or tasks, and it can seem like their mind is elsewhere. This detachment was evident in Lily when she would zone out during conversations or seem unresponsive to her surroundings, a clear indication that she was struggling internally.

Changes in sleep patterns can be another crucial indicator. PTSD often affects a child's ability to sleep soundly. Nightmares, difficulty falling asleep, or frequent waking during the night can all be signs of trauma. Lily had trouble sleeping through the night, often waking up in a panic or unable to return to sleep. This lack of restful sleep only compounded her anxiety and emotional struggles during the day.

Physical symptoms like frequent headaches or stomachaches can also be linked to emotional distress. These complaints may not always have a clear medical cause but can be a manifestation of the child's emotional turmoil. Lily's recurring physical complaints were often tied to her feelings of anxiety and stress, further complicating her ability to manage her trauma.

As a parent, being vigilant and empathetic towards these behavioral and emotional indicators is key. It involves creating an open line of communication where your child feels safe to express their feelings and fears. Encourage them to talk about their emotions and experiences, and reassure them that it's okay to feel the way they do. Provide a stable and supportive environment where they can express themselves without judgment.

Seeking professional help is also an important step. A mental health professional specializing in trauma can offer valuable insights and therapeutic strategies to help your child manage their PTSD symptoms. This professional support, combined with your understanding and patience, can make a significant difference in your child's journey toward healing.

By being aware of these behavioral and emotional indicators and responding with compassion and support, you can help your child navigate through their trauma and work towards a healthier, more balanced emotional state. Recognizing and addressing these signs early can pave the way for effective intervention and long-term recovery.

Differences between typical childhood behaviors and PTSD symptoms

Understanding the difference between typical childhood behaviors and symptoms of PTSD is crucial for effectively supporting a child dealing with trauma. As a parent, distinguishing between everyday developmental changes and signs of PTSD can help you provide appropriate responses and seek timely intervention. Here's a detailed look at how these two can differ and overlap, illustrated with practical insights.

Children naturally go through various behavioral phases as they grow. These can include temper tantrums, mood swings, and periods of withdrawal, all of which can be part of normal development. However, when these behaviors are linked to PTSD, they take on a different intensity and frequency, reflecting deeper emotional distress.

Typical Childhood Behaviors

1. Mood Swings: It's common for children to experience mood swings as they navigate social and emotional challenges. For instance, a child might have a tantrum because they can't have a toy or because they're tired. These mood swings are usually short-lived and related to immediate frustrations or unmet needs.

2. Separation Anxiety: Young children often experience separation anxiety when starting school or being away from their primary caregivers. This anxiety typically decreases as they adjust to new routines and gain confidence.

3. Curiosity and Imagination: Children frequently engage in imaginative play and may have fears related to their fantasies or play scenarios. This is a normal part of cognitive development and usually doesn't interfere with their daily functioning.

4. Occasional Withdrawal: It's typical for children to withdraw from social interactions occasionally, especially when they're tired or overstimulated. This temporary withdrawal is usually reversible and not indicative of a deeper issue.

PTSD Symptoms

1. Intense and Persistent Fear: Unlike typical childhood fears, PTSD-related fears are intense and pervasive. A child with PTSD might have severe anxiety about situations that seem benign to others, such as loud noises or certain people, reflecting their trauma rather than normal developmental stages.

2. Recurrent Nightmares or Flashbacks: While occasional nightmares are common in childhood, children with PTSD experience frequent, distressing nightmares or flashbacks that are directly related to their traumatic experience. These can disrupt their sleep and affect their daily functioning.

3. Exaggerated Startle Responses: PTSD often leads to an exaggerated startle response. A child might jump or react intensely to sudden noises or movements, showing a heightened state of alertness that goes beyond typical childhood reactions.

4. Persistent Withdrawal: While temporary withdrawal is normal, persistent social withdrawal in a child with PTSD is a cause for concern. This can manifest as an ongoing reluctance to engage with family, friends, or activities, reflecting deeper emotional pain and avoidance behaviors.

5. Significant Behavioral Changes: Behavioral changes in PTSD are more profound and disruptive. For instance, a child might display aggressive behavior or sudden outbursts that are disproportionate to the situation, showing that their emotional regulation is severely impacted by their trauma.

As a parent, it's essential to observe not just the behavior but also the context and duration of these symptoms. Typical childhood behaviors usually resolve over time with minimal intervention, while PTSD symptoms often persist and worsen without appropriate support. If you notice that a child's behavior is intense, persistent, and affecting their daily life, it might indicate PTSD rather than just normal developmental changes.

Understanding these differences helps in providing the right support and seeking professional help when necessary. A mental health professional can offer a thorough assessment and develop a tailored treatment plan to address the specific needs of a child dealing with PTSD. By differentiating between typical behaviors and PTSD symptoms, you can ensure that your child receives the appropriate care and support they need to heal and thrive.

Guidelines for assessing when professional help is needed

Knowing when to seek professional help for your child with PTSD can be challenging. As a parent, it's essential to recognize the signs that indicate your child's needs go beyond what can be managed at home. Here are practical guidelines to help you assess when it's time to involve a mental health professional.

Persistent and Severe Symptoms

If your child's symptoms persist for an extended period or become more severe, it may be time to seek professional help. For example, if nightmares, flashbacks, or intense fears continue despite your efforts to comfort and reassure them, it suggests that their trauma is deeply affecting their daily life. Symptoms that interfere significantly with their ability to function at school, in social settings, or at home are especially concerning.

When my daughter struggled with persistent nightmares and frequent panic attacks that seemed unmanageable, it was a sign that we needed professional intervention. Despite trying various strategies at home, her symptoms remained severe and disruptive, making it clear that specialized help was required.

Impairment in Daily Functioning

Professional help is warranted when PTSD symptoms begin to impair your child's ability to perform daily activities. This includes difficulties with schoolwork, trouble interacting with peers, or a decline in personal hygiene. For instance, if your child shows a marked decrease in academic performance or withdraws from friends and family to the extent that it affects their social development, it indicates a level of distress that may benefit from professional support.

When Lily started showing a decline in her school performance and became increasingly isolated from her friends, it was evident that her trauma was impacting her overall well-being. This was a clear indicator that additional support was necessary.

Ineffective Coping Strategies

If the coping strategies you are using at home are not providing relief or if they seem to be causing additional distress, it's time to consult a professional. Effective strategies for managing PTSD symptoms often require a combination of approaches, including therapy and sometimes medication. If your attempts to help your child feel secure and manage their emotions aren't working, a mental health professional can offer new techniques and therapies that might be more effective.

For example, despite using various calming techniques and establishing routines at home, if Lily's anxiety and fear did not improve, it was a signal that professional guidance could offer new approaches and interventions that we hadn't yet explored.

Escalation of Behavioral Issues

When behavioral issues associated with PTSD escalate or become unmanageable, seeking professional help is crucial. This includes severe aggression, self-harm, or extreme withdrawal. If you notice that your child is engaging in harmful behaviors or showing a significant increase in aggression, it's essential to get professional support to address these serious issues.

In Lily's case, as her outbursts of anger became more frequent and intense, it was clear that these behaviors were beyond what could be managed with typical parenting strategies alone. This escalation was a strong indication that professional assistance was needed.

Concerns About Safety

If you have concerns about your child's safety or if they express thoughts of self-harm or harming others, immediate professional help is necessary. Safety is the highest priority, and mental health professionals can provide the appropriate interventions to ensure your child's well-being.

When Lily's anxiety reached a point where she began expressing fears about harming herself or others, it was an urgent call to seek professional intervention. Safety concerns must be addressed immediately to protect your child and ensure they receive the appropriate care.

Uncertainty and Feeling Overwhelmed

If you, as a parent, feel uncertain about how to help your child or overwhelmed by the situation, seeking professional advice can provide clarity and support. Mental health professionals can offer guidance, reassurance, and resources to help you navigate your child's needs effectively.

In my experience, feeling overwhelmed by the complexity of Lily's symptoms made it clear that professional help was not just beneficial but necessary. The support and expertise of a mental health professional provided the reassurance and direction we needed.

By keeping these guidelines in mind, you can make informed decisions about when to seek professional help for your child with PTSD. Ensuring that your child receives the appropriate care and support is crucial for their healing and overall well-being. Remember, seeking help is a proactive step towards providing the best possible support for your child.

Steps to take when seeking help

(e.g., finding a therapist, making appointments)

Navigating the journey to find professional help for your child with PTSD can feel overwhelming. It's a path that involves finding the right therapist and understanding the steps needed to access their support. Here's a guide to help you through this process and ensure you find the best assistance for your child.

Start by identifying the right type of mental health professional for your child. Psychologists, psychiatrists, and licensed therapists each play a unique role in treating PTSD. Psychologists often focus on therapy and counseling to help your child manage their trauma. Psychiatrists can diagnose PTSD and prescribe medication if needed, usually handling more complex cases or those requiring medication. Licensed therapists, including clinical social workers, marriage and family therapists, and counselors, offer various therapies, such as cognitive-behavioral therapy (CBT) and trauma-focused therapy. Choose a professional who specializes in trauma and PTSD in children based on your child's specific needs.

Once you know the type of professional needed, begin your search. You can start by asking your pediatrician, family doctor, or trusted friends and family for recommendations. They might know reputable therapists who specialize in PTSD. Additionally, check with your health insurance provider for a list of covered mental health professionals to manage costs effectively. Professional associations, like the American Psychological Association (APA) or the National Association of

Social Workers (NASW), also have directories of licensed practitioners.

With a list of potential therapists, it's important to evaluate each one to find the best fit for your child. Look for therapists with experience in treating children with PTSD. Their background and specialized training can make a significant difference in the effectiveness of their treatment. Research their therapeutic approach to ensure it aligns with your child's needs. Some therapists use trauma-focused therapy, while others may have different methods. Also, consider if the therapist has experience with children of your child's age and if their style seems approachable and empathetic, as the therapeutic relationship is crucial for successful treatment.

After selecting a potential therapist, schedule an appointment. Contact the therapist's office to check availability and set up an initial consultation. This first meeting helps you assess whether the therapist is a good fit for your child. Prepare a list of questions to ask during the consultation, such as their experience, treatment methods, and how they involve parents in the therapy process. Confirm the details of the appointment, including location, duration, necessary paperwork, and costs.

Before the first appointment, prepare both your child and yourself. Explain to your child what to expect during therapy using simple and reassuring language. Let them know that the therapist is there to help them feel better. Gather any relevant information about your child's trauma history, behavior, and previous treatments to provide the therapist with a complete picture. Discuss your goals for therapy with the therapist to help guide the treatment process.

After starting therapy, regularly assess how it's going. Observe your child's response to the therapist and any changes in their symptoms. Provide feedback to the therapist about what's working and any concerns you have. Open communication is key to tailoring the treatment to your child's needs. Be open to making adjustments if necessary. If the initial therapist isn't the right fit, don't hesitate to seek another professional.

By following these steps, you can navigate the process of seeking professional help more confidently. Finding the right therapist and ensuring your child gets the support they need is a crucial step in their healing journey. Your proactive approach in seeking help will play a significant role in your child's recovery and overall well-being.

Chapter 3
Effective Communication Strategies

Talking to a child about their feelings and experiences, especially when they have PTSD, can be challenging. It's crucial to approach these conversations with care to ensure your child feels safe and heard. Here's a detailed approach to doing this effectively:

Creating a Safe Space

Start by setting up a calm, comfortable environment for your discussions. Choose a quiet spot where you won't be interrupted. This could be a cozy corner of your home, a special chair, or any place where your child feels at ease. The key is to make sure it's a space where they feel relaxed and secure.

Ensure your body language and tone are reassuring. Sit at your child's level to make the interaction more personal and less intimidating. Maintain a gentle and patient demeanor to help them feel comfortable opening up.

Using Simple and Gentle Language

When initiating a conversation, use words that are appropriate for your child's age and understanding. For instance, instead of asking, **"Can you describe what happened?"** try saying, **"Can you tell me what's been on your mind recently?"** This way, you invite them to share without putting too much pressure on them.

Avoid complex questions that might overwhelm your child. Instead, keep your questions open-ended and straightforward to help them express their feelings without feeling intimidated.

Listening Actively

Active listening is essential for effective communication. Focus completely on your child when they talk. This means putting away distractions, making eye contact, and showing that you are genuinely interested in what they have to say.

Show empathy through your responses. Use small verbal affirmations like **"I understand"** or **"That sounds really hard"** to let them know you are engaged. Avoid interrupting them or jumping in with solutions too quickly. Sometimes, they just need to talk through their feelings and might not be looking for immediate answers.

Encouraging Use of Their Own Words

Help your child articulate their emotions by asking open-ended questions such as, **"How did that make you feel?"** or **"What was going through your mind when that happened?"** Avoid labeling their feelings for them. Instead, let them express their emotions in their own words. This helps them feel more in control of their experience and validates their feelings.

Being Patient with Emotions

Children with PTSD may express their feelings in various ways, including anger, sadness, or silence. Be patient and prepared for a range of emotions. If your child becomes upset, stay calm and offer comfort. Reassure them that it's okay to feel whatever they are feeling and that you are there to support them. Your calmness will help them feel secure and understood.

Using Positive Reinforcement

Praise your child for sharing their feelings, no matter how small. Positive reinforcement helps build their confidence and encourages them to continue expressing themselves. For example, you might say, **"I'm really glad you told me how you're feeling. It's important for us to talk about these things."**

Incorporating Creative Methods

For younger children or those who find verbal communication difficult, consider using creative methods like drawing or storytelling. These activities can help your child express their feelings in a non-verbal way. Let them guide the process and interpret their expressions, providing support and understanding based on what they share.

Focusing on What They Can Control

When discussing their feelings, talk about strategies they can use to manage their emotions. Simple techniques like deep breathing, finding a comforting object, or using a calming routine can be helpful. Encourage your child to identify what makes them feel better and incorporate these strategies into their daily life.

Being Consistent

Make communication a regular part of your routine. Regularly check in with your child about their feelings and experiences. This helps maintain an open line of dialogue and reassures them that they can always come to you with their concerns.

Seeking Professional Help

If conversations become too challenging or if your child's reactions are intense, don't hesitate to seek professional help. Therapists and counselors can provide additional strategies and support for navigating these discussions effectively.

By using these techniques, you can help your child feel more comfortable talking about their feelings and experiences. Effective communication supports their emotional healing and strengthens your relationship with them.

Methods to Foster Open, Honest Dialogue

Creating a space where your child feels comfortable sharing their thoughts and feelings is crucial, especially when they are dealing with PTSD. Here are some effective methods to foster open, honest dialogue with your child:

Be Approachable and Available

Let your child know that they can come to you anytime to talk. Your availability and openness are key. A simple, reassuring statement like, **"I'm here whenever you need to talk about anything,"** can make a significant difference. It shows your child that they have a safe and judgment-free space to express themselves.

Use Active Listening Techniques

Active listening is more than just hearing words; it involves showing genuine interest in your child's thoughts and feelings. When your child speaks, give them your full attention. Avoid distractions such as phones or computers. Use body language like nodding and maintaining eye contact to show you are engaged. Reflect back what you hear to confirm understanding. For example, if your child says, **"I don't want to go to school,"** you might respond with, **"It sounds like you're feeling worried about school. Can you tell me more about what's on your mind?"**

Establish a Routine for Conversations

Creating a routine for conversations helps normalize discussing feelings. Set aside regular times each day or week for check-ins. For instance, you might have a bedtime routine where you spend a few minutes talking about the day's events or how your child is feeling. This consistency helps your child see that talking about feelings is a normal and important part of their daily life.

Ask Open-Ended Questions

Encourage your child to share more about their thoughts and feelings by asking open-ended questions. These are questions that require more than a simple **"yes"** or **"no"** answer. For example, instead of asking, **"Did you have a good day?"** ask, "What was the most interesting part of your day?" Open-ended questions help your child explore their feelings in more depth and provide you with better insights into their experiences.

Be Mindful of Tone and Body Language

Your tone of voice and body language can greatly influence how comfortable your child feels. Maintain a calm and reassuring tone, and use open body language, such as leaning slightly forward and avoiding crossed arms. These non-verbal cues show that you are engaged and supportive, making your child feel more at ease.

Validate Your Child's Feelings

Acknowledging and validating your child's emotions is essential. Let them know that their feelings are legitimate and important. For instance, if your child expresses frustration, you might say, **"I can see that you're feeling frustrated. It's okay to feel that way. Let's talk about what's been going on."** Validation helps your child feel understood and supports them in opening up more.

Be Patient and Give Them Time

Children may need time to gather their thoughts and express themselves. Avoid rushing them or pressing them for answers before they're ready. Allow them to take their time and express their feelings at their own pace. Your patience shows that you respect their process and are willing to wait for them to feel comfortable.

Incorporate Activities That Promote Conversation

Sometimes, engaging in a shared activity can make it easier for your child to talk. Activities like playing a game, going for a walk, or even cooking together can provide a relaxed environment where your child might feel more comfortable sharing their thoughts and feelings.

Model Open Communication

Show your child how to express feelings by sharing your own experiences and emotions in an age-appropriate way. For example, you might say, "I felt a bit stressed today because of work, but talking about it with you helped me feel better. How about you? Is there anything you'd like to talk about?" Modeling open communication demonstrates that talking about feelings is normal and helps your child feel more comfortable doing the same.

By implementing these methods, you create a supportive environment where your child feels encouraged to share their thoughts and emotions. Open and honest dialogue is crucial for helping your child navigate their feelings and build a strong, supportive relationship with you.

Active Listening Skills and Empathetic Responses

Active listening and empathetic responses are fundamental in building a strong and supportive communication channel with your child, especially when dealing with PTSD. These skills not only help you understand your child's feelings more deeply but also provide the emotional support they need. Here's how to effectively apply these skills:

Give Your Full Attention

When your child is speaking, it's essential to give them your undivided attention. Put away distractions such as phones or computers and focus entirely on what your child is saying. Maintain eye contact and use body language, like nodding and leaning slightly forward, to show that you are fully present. This attentiveness communicates that their words are important to you.

Avoid Interrupting

Let your child finish their thoughts before you respond. Interrupting can make them feel that their feelings are not valued or that they need to rush through their thoughts. Allowing them to express themselves fully shows respect for their perspective and helps build trust between you.

Reflect Back What You Hear

Reflective listening involves paraphrasing or summarizing what your child has said to confirm your understanding. For example, if your child says, "**I feel like nobody understands what I'm going through,**" you might respond with, "**It sounds like you feel really alone in what you're experiencing.**" This approach not only demonstrates that you're attentive but also affirms their emotions, making them feel understood.

Use Open-Ended Questions

Encourage your child to explore their thoughts and feelings more deeply by asking open-ended questions. These questions require more than a simple "**yes**" or "**no**" answer and prompt detailed responses. Instead of asking, "**Are you feeling sad?**" ask, "**Can you tell me more about what's making you feel sad?**" This approach helps your child articulate their emotions and provides you with better insight into their experiences.

Show Empathy

Empathy involves recognizing and validating your child's emotions, even if you don't fully understand them. For instance, if your child is upset about a situation, you might say, "**I can see that you're feeling really upset right now. It must be really hard for you.**" By empathizing with their feelings, you provide comfort and support, showing that you understand and care about their emotional state.

Respond with Compassion and Reassurance

When your child expresses their feelings, focus on providing comfort rather than offering quick fixes or solutions. For example, if your child is anxious about an upcoming event, you might say, **"I understand that you're feeling anxious. It's okay to feel that way. We can talk about what's making you nervous and find ways to help you feel better."** Compassionate responses help your child feel supported and less alone in their struggles.

Be Patient and Give Time

Children may need time to articulate their feelings or might struggle to find the right words. Avoid pressuring them to speak quickly or provide answers immediately. Instead, allow them the time they need to express themselves and offer gentle encouragement if needed. Your patience shows respect for their process and helps build a trusting relationship.

Encourage Non-Verbal Expression

Some children may find it easier to express their emotions through drawing, writing, or other forms of creative expression. Support these methods and engage with them to gain insight into their feelings. For example, if your child draws a picture about their feelings, discuss what the drawing represents and use it as a starting point for further conversation.

Avoid Judgment and Unsolicited Advice

During conversations, focus on listening and understanding rather than offering unsolicited advice or making judgments. If your child shares something difficult, resist the urge to immediately solve the problem or tell them how they should feel. Instead, provide a supportive and non-judgmental space for them to express their emotions.

Regularly Check In

Even if your child isn't actively talking about their PTSD, regular check-ins show that you care and are available for support. Ask open-ended questions and provide opportunities for them to share when they're ready. Regularly checking in helps maintain an open line of communication and reinforces your role as a supportive presence in their life.

By practicing active listening and responding with empathy, you create a supportive environment that encourages open communication and strengthens your connection with your child. These skills not only help in understanding their current struggles but also lay the groundwork for ongoing support and trust.

Ways to Encourage Children to Express Their Thoughts and Emotions

Encouraging your child to express their thoughts and emotions, especially when they're dealing with PTSD, requires a thoughtful and supportive approach. From my own experience as a parent, I've found several effective strategies to help create an environment where my child feels comfortable sharing their feelings. Here's how you can encourage your child to open up:

Create a Safe and Welcoming Space

A comforting environment is crucial for encouraging your child to share their emotions. At home, I've established a cozy corner where my child feels secure and at ease. This space isn't just about physical comfort but also about fostering an atmosphere where feelings are respected and heard. Setting aside regular time for conversations, even if it's just a few minutes each day, helps show your child that their thoughts and feelings are valued.

Model Emotional Expression

Children often look to their parents for cues on how to handle their own feelings. By openly sharing my own emotions and discussing how I manage them, I've helped my child understand that expressing feelings is both normal and healthy. For example, I might say, **"I'm feeling a bit stressed today because of work, but talking about it helps me feel better. If you're feeling something, talking might help you too."**

Incorporate Creative Activities

Creative activities can be a wonderful way for children to express their emotions. For my child, drawing, writing, and playing music have been effective outlets for their feelings. I provide various art supplies and encourage my child to use them to express what's inside. Even if they can't find the right words, these creative methods allow them to communicate their emotions in a different way.

Use Books and Stories

Books and stories can open up conversations about emotions. Reading about characters who experience feelings similar to what my child is going through often leads to discussions about their own experiences. For instance, discussing a story where a character faces challenges can prompt my child to reflect on their own feelings and share more about their personal experiences.

Ask Open-Ended Questions

Open-ended questions encourage deeper exploration of feelings. Instead of asking questions that can be answered with a simple **"yes"** or **"no,"** I ask questions that invite more detailed responses. For example, **"What was the best part of your day?"** or "Can you tell me about a time when you felt really happy or sad?" These questions encourage my child to reflect more deeply on their experiences and express their emotions more thoroughly.

Use Feelings Charts or Emotion Wheels

For younger children or those who find it hard to articulate their feelings, feelings charts or emotion wheels can be useful tools. These visual aids list or picture various emotions, allowing children to point to or discuss how they're feeling. It's been a gentle and effective way for my child to communicate their emotions and for us to have meaningful conversations about them.

Encourage Routine Check-Ins

Having regular **"feelings check-ins"** has been beneficial in our home. At the end of each day, we talk about our highs and lows, which helps keep us connected and aware of each other's emotional states. This routine has normalized talking about feelings and made it a natural part of our day.

Affirm and Validate Feelings

When my child shares their emotions, I make sure to acknowledge and validate their feelings. For example, I might say, **"It sounds like you're feeling really frustrated right now, and that's okay. It's important to feel and talk about these things."** Validation helps my child feel understood and supports their emotional expression.

By using these methods, I've seen my child become more comfortable with expressing their emotions. Every child is unique, so it may take time to discover what works best for your family. Patience, consistency, and a loving approach are key. Encouraging emotional expression not only helps your child cope with PTSD but also strengthens your relationship and fosters a deeper understanding between you both.

Chapter 4
Creating a Safe Environment

Creating a trauma-informed environment is essential for helping your child with PTSD feel safe and supported. This approach is all about understanding how trauma affects your child and making adjustments to your home and interactions that can help them heal. Here's a detailed guide to building such an environment.

Understanding Trauma-Informed Care

A trauma-informed environment starts with understanding what trauma is and how it impacts children. Trauma can affect a child's brain, emotions, and behavior. It can make them feel anxious, scared, or detached. To support your child effectively, you need to be aware of these impacts and approach their needs with sensitivity and compassion.

Creating a Sense of Safety

Safety is the foundation of a trauma-informed environment. It's crucial that your child feels secure in their surroundings. Begin by ensuring that your home is a place where they can relax and feel protected. This means addressing any potential sources of stress or fear, such as loud noises, unpredictable routines, or unsafe areas.

Create a calming space where your child can retreat when they feel overwhelmed. This could be a cozy corner with soft pillows, calming colors, and comforting objects. Having a designated safe space gives your child a place to go when they need to calm down or feel secure.

Consistency and Routine

Children with PTSD often find comfort in predictability. Consistent routines and clear expectations can help them feel more in control and less anxious. Establish regular daily routines for activities like meals, bedtime, and homework. When your child knows what to expect, it can reduce their stress and help them feel more stable.

Consistency also means being reliable in your interactions with your child. This includes following through on promises, maintaining calmness in stressful situations, and being dependable. Your child will benefit from knowing they can trust you and that their environment is predictable.

Open Communication

Open communication is another key element of a trauma-informed environment. Encourage your child to express their feelings and thoughts, and listen to them without judgment. Let them know it's okay to talk about their fears or concerns. Use simple and reassuring language when discussing difficult topics, and avoid pressuring them to share more than they're comfortable with.

Create opportunities for your child to communicate through various methods, not just talking. Drawing, writing, or using play can help them express what they're feeling if they have trouble putting their emotions into words.

Empathy and Understanding

Showing empathy and understanding is vital in a trauma-informed environment. Recognize that your child's reactions and behaviors are a result of their trauma, not intentional defiance. Approach their behavior with patience and compassion, and try to understand what might be triggering their distress.

Validate their feelings, even if they seem exaggerated or irrational to you. Let your child know that their emotions are important and that it's okay to feel what they're feeling. Your supportive responses will help them build trust and feel more secure.

Respecting Boundaries

Respecting your child's boundaries is essential. Trauma can make children feel vulnerable, so it's important to be mindful of their personal space and preferences. Avoid pushing them to engage in activities or conversations they're not ready for. Instead, let them take the lead and only engage when they're comfortable.

Encourage them to set boundaries and respect those boundaries yourself. This helps them learn to advocate for their needs and understand that their feelings are valued.

Promoting Positive Reinforcement

Positive reinforcement can be a powerful tool in a trauma-informed environment. Celebrate your child's efforts and achievements, no matter how small. Recognize and praise their progress, and provide encouragement when they face challenges. This helps build their self-esteem and reinforces positive behavior.

Use rewards and praise to motivate and support your child. Make sure the reinforcement is meaningful to them, and tailor it to their interests and preferences. Positive reinforcement helps create a nurturing environment that supports their healing and growth.

Training and Support for Caregivers
Building a trauma-informed environment also involves ensuring that everyone involved in your child's care is knowledgeable and supportive. This means educating yourself and others in your child's life about PTSD and trauma. Attend workshops, read books, and seek advice from professionals to better understand how to support your child effectively.

Encourage other caregivers, such as family members or teachers, to learn about trauma-informed care. This ensures a consistent approach to your child's needs and creates a supportive network that can contribute to their healing process.

Creating a trauma-informed environment is an ongoing process. It requires patience, understanding, and a commitment to meeting your child's needs with sensitivity. By building a safe, supportive, and empathetic environment, you can help your child navigate their trauma and move towards a path of healing and resilience.

Importance of Consistency, Routines, and Stability

Creating a stable and predictable environment is crucial for children with PTSD. It helps them feel safe and secure, which can significantly ease their anxiety and promote healing. Let's explore practical strategies for establishing and maintaining consistency, routines, and stability in your home.

Establishing Effective Routines

Routines provide structure and predictability, which are essential for children dealing with PTSD. To create a routine that works for your child, start by identifying key activities that occur daily or weekly. These might include wake-up times, meals, school or activity schedules, bedtime routines, and family time.

1. **Create Visual Schedules**: Visual schedules can be incredibly helpful for children with PTSD. Use pictures or drawings to represent daily activities. Hang the schedule in a common area where your child can easily see it. This visual aid helps your child understand what to expect throughout the day, reducing anxiety about transitions.

2. **Involve Your Child:** When setting up routines, involve your child in the process. This inclusion can make them feel more in control and less anxious about changes. Let them choose or suggest parts of the routine that are important to them, such as the order of activities or special tasks they can help with.

3. Use Checklists: For older children, checklists can be a useful tool. Create a checklist for daily tasks like getting ready for school or bedtime preparations. Checking off items can give your child a sense of accomplishment and clarity about what needs to be done.

Maintaining Consistency

Consistency in your responses and actions provides a sense of predictability that can be very comforting for a child with PTSD. Here's how you can maintain consistency:

1. Stick to the Routine: As much as possible, follow the established routines. Consistency helps reinforce a sense of safety and control. If changes are necessary, prepare your child in advance and explain the reasons behind them.

2. Consistent Responses to Behavior: Be consistent in how you respond to your child's behavior. If certain behaviors are addressed with specific consequences, make sure these are applied consistently. This helps your child understand what is expected and reduces confusion or anxiety about potential responses.

3. Address Disruptions Calmly: Sometimes, disruptions to routines are unavoidable. When they occur, approach them calmly and provide reassurance to your child. Explain how you'll manage the disruption and what steps you're taking to return to the routine as soon as possible.

Creating a Stable Environment

Beyond daily routines, stability involves creating a secure and supportive home environment:

1. Foster Reliable Relationships: Encourage regular, positive interactions with family members and trusted adults. Reliable relationships help build trust and offer emotional support. Consistent engagement and open communication with family can provide a steady source of comfort.

2. Predictable Interactions: Try to maintain a consistent approach in your interactions with your child. Use a calm and reassuring tone, and be predictable in your responses to their needs. This predictability helps your child feel more secure.

3. Create Safe Spaces: Designate a safe space in your home where your child can retreat when feeling overwhelmed. This space should be calming and comforting, with items that help your child feel secure, like soft pillows, favorite toys, or soothing music.

Addressing Common Challenges

Maintaining consistency and routines can be challenging, especially when dealing with disruptions or changes. Here's how to handle common issues:

1. Managing Unexpected Changes: When unexpected changes arise, communicate with your child about what's happening and how it will affect the routine. Offer reassurance and support during transitions to help them adjust.

2. Dealing with Resistance: If your child resists the established routine, try to understand their concerns and work through them together. Adjust the routine as needed to address their needs while maintaining overall structure.

3. Adapting Routines: Routines should be flexible enough to adapt to your child's evolving needs. Regularly review and adjust the routine as necessary to ensure it continues to meet your child's needs and provides the stability they require.

By focusing on these strategies, you can create a nurturing and supportive environment that promotes your child's well-being and helps them manage their PTSD symptoms more effectively. The consistency, routines, and stability you provide are crucial components of their healing journey.

Creating physical and emotional safety

Creating both physical and emotional safety is crucial for nurturing a child with PTSD. These elements are vital for establishing a secure environment that supports your child's healing and well-being. Here's how to foster safety in both areas. To ensure physical safety, start by securing your home environment. Remove potential hazards such as sharp objects and electrical outlets. Make sure your child's sleeping area is comfortable and free from dangers, and consider using a nightlight if they are afraid of the dark. A calming bedtime routine can also contribute to their sense of safety. If your child uses digital devices, implement parental controls and monitor their online activities to protect them from harmful content or interactions.

Emotional safety is equally important and involves creating a space where your child feels valued, understood, and supported. Open and honest communication is key. Make sure your child knows they can express their feelings without fear of judgment. Consistency in communication reinforces trust and security. Validate your child's emotions, even when they seem intense or challenging. Let them know their feelings are important and it's okay to express them. Regular reassurance of their safety and love helps build emotional security and resilience.

A supportive environment involves both physical and emotional aspects working together. Foster positive interactions within the family by promoting respectful and supportive relationships. Encourage activities that build strong, trusting bonds, such as family games and shared hobbies. Clearly define and communicate boundaries and expectations. Consistent rules and guidelines provide structure and security. Help your child feel a sense of belonging by celebrating their achievements and including them in family activities. This sense of belonging reinforces their emotional safety and boosts their confidence.

Addressing challenges in safety involves handling specific safety concerns promptly, such as fixing hazards or adjusting the home environment. If your child has strong emotional responses, approach them with empathy and support. Use calming techniques and provide a safe space for them to express their feelings. Seek professional help if needed to address ongoing emotional challenges. Be prepared to adapt safety measures as your child grows and their needs change.

Regularly review and adjust strategies to ensure they meet your child's evolving needs.

By focusing on both physical and emotional safety, you create a nurturing environment that supports your child's healing and well-being. This comprehensive approach builds a strong foundation of security and trust, essential for managing PTSD and promoting positive growth.

Managing stress and anxiety within the home

Managing stress and anxiety within the home is essential for creating a supportive environment for a child with PTSD. Building on the foundation of a trauma-informed environment, consistency, and safety, here's how to address stress and anxiety in a nurturing way.

Start by establishing routines that help reduce stress. Consistent schedules for daily activities, such as mealtimes, homework, and bedtime, provide structure and predictability, which can ease anxiety. Knowing what to expect each day can make your child feel more secure and less overwhelmed. Encourage your child to participate in these routines, giving them a sense of control and involvement.

Create a calm and supportive atmosphere in your home. This involves not just physical safety but also emotional reassurance. Designate quiet, relaxing spaces where your child can go to unwind when they feel overwhelmed. Use calming techniques like deep breathing exercises, progressive muscle relaxation, or mindfulness practices to help manage stress. Teach these techniques to your child and model them yourself to show that handling stress is a normal part of life.

Address sources of stress proactively. Observe what triggers your child's anxiety and work to minimize these stressors. For example, if schoolwork is causing stress, consider setting up a quiet, organized study area and providing extra support with their assignments. If social situations are overwhelming, discuss strategies to handle them and offer support in navigating these experiences.

Encourage open communication about feelings. Let your child know that it's okay to talk about their worries and that you are there to listen and support them. Regular family meetings can provide a space to discuss any concerns and share feelings. Validate their experiences and feelings, showing empathy and understanding. Reinforce that they are not alone and that it's okay to ask for help when needed.

Managing stress also involves self-care for the entire family. Stress affects everyone, so ensure that all family members take time for their own well-being. Engage in activities that you enjoy, and make time for relaxation and self-care. Model healthy stress management techniques for your child, as they often learn by observing the adults around them.

If your child's stress and anxiety are persistent or worsening, seeking professional support may be necessary. A mental health professional can provide tailored strategies and therapies to help manage these symptoms more effectively. Work closely with them to ensure that their recommendations are integrated into your home environment.

By integrating these practices into your daily life, you contribute to a home environment that effectively manages stress and anxiety. This supportive approach, grounded in consistency, safety, and open communication, helps your child feel more secure and better able to cope with the challenges of PTSD.

Practical tips for making the home a place of security and comfort

Creating a home environment that feels secure and comforting is crucial for supporting a child with PTSD. Building on the foundation of a trauma-informed environment, consistency, safety, and stress management, here are practical tips to make your home a haven of security and comfort.

Start by personalizing your child's space to make it feel like their own. Allow them to choose colors, decorations, and items that make them feel comfortable and safe. This personal touch can provide a sense of ownership and security. If possible, create a cozy corner where they can retreat when feeling overwhelmed. This might include their favorite blanket, stuffed animals, or a soft chair. A space like this helps them feel grounded and safe.

Maintain a calm and soothing atmosphere throughout your home. Use gentle lighting, soft colors, and comfortable furnishings to create a relaxing environment. Reduce noise and avoid overstimulation, which can be distressing for a child with PTSD. Soft music, white noise machines, or calming nature sounds can help create a peaceful ambiance.

Incorporate comforting routines into daily life. Establish rituals that provide stability and reassurance, such as reading a favorite book before bed, having a regular family meal, or engaging in a calming bedtime routine. These routines offer predictability and comfort, helping your child feel more secure.

Encourage positive interactions and family bonding. Spend quality time together engaging in activities that bring joy and relaxation, such as playing games, cooking, or going for walks. Building strong, positive connections within the family enhances feelings of security and support. Show affection and provide reassurance regularly, reinforcing that your child is loved and valued.

Address any practical needs that contribute to a sense of security. Make sure your home is secure and without dangers. Childproof areas that might be risky and ensure that your child knows what to do in case of an emergency. Discuss emergency plans with them in a way that feels reassuring rather than frightening. Knowing there is a plan can help reduce anxiety.

Teach and model self-care practices. Encourage your child to engage in activities that promote relaxation and well-being, such as hobbies, physical exercise, and healthy eating. Demonstrate self-care by taking time for your own well-being and showing how to handle stress in healthy ways. This not only supports your child's emotional health but also reinforces the importance of taking care of oneself.

Create a supportive network. Connect with other parents, support groups, or community resources that can provide additional support and advice. Sometimes, knowing that others share similar experiences can offer comfort and practical tips for managing daily challenges.

Lastly, remain flexible and patient. Understand that creating a secure and comforting environment is an ongoing process. Be open to making adjustments as your child's needs evolve and as you learn more about what helps them feel safe and supported. Regularly check in with your child to see how they are feeling and what might make their environment more comforting for them.

By implementing these practical tips, you can create a home environment that feels secure and comforting for your child. This nurturing space helps them feel safe, supported, and valued, providing a strong foundation for their healing journey.

Chapter 5
Supporting Emotional Regulation

Understanding and managing emotions can be challenging for children, especially those dealing with PTSD. As parents, helping your child learn to regulate and express their emotions in healthy ways is crucial for their overall well-being and recovery. Here are some practical techniques to support your child in developing emotional regulation skills.

Start with Simple Breathing Exercises. Teaching your child how to use their breath to calm down can be incredibly effective. Deep breathing helps to slow down the heart rate and relax the body, which can reduce feelings of anxiety and stress. Show your child how to take slow, deep breaths: inhale through the nose for a count of four, hold for a count of four, and then exhale through the mouth for a count of four. You can make this exercise fun by using a favorite stuffed animal or a toy. Have your child place the toy on their stomach and watch it rise and fall as they breathe. Practicing this regularly can help them feel more in control during stressful moments.

Introduce Grounding Techniques. Grounding techniques are useful for bringing a child back to the present moment when they feel overwhelmed or disconnected. One simple grounding technique is the 5-4-3-2-1 exercise, where the child identifies five things they can see, four things they can touch, three things they can hear, two things they can smell, and one thing they can taste. This technique helps them focus on their immediate surroundings and can reduce feelings of panic or dissociation.

Encourage Journaling. Writing in a journal offers children a secure place to share their thoughts and emotions. Encourage your child to write or draw about their experiences, emotions, and thoughts. You can start by asking them simple questions like, **"What made you happy today?"** or **"What was the hardest part of your day?"** If your child finds writing difficult, drawing can also be a powerful way for them to express themselves. Journaling helps children process their emotions and gain insight into their feelings.

Use Visual Aids for Emotional Expression. Visual aids, such as emotion charts or mood meters, can help children identify and articulate their emotions. Create a simple chart with different facial expressions representing various emotions like happiness, sadness, anger, and fear. Encourage your child to point to or describe how they're feeling using the chart. This can be particularly helpful for younger children or those who struggle with verbal expression.

Model Healthy Emotional Responses. Children learn a lot from observing their parents. By demonstrating healthy ways to manage and express your own emotions, you provide your child with a powerful example to follow. Show them how you handle stress, frustration, or sadness in a constructive manner. For instance, if you're feeling upset, you might say, "I'm feeling frustrated right now, so I'm going to take a few deep breaths to help me calm down." This not only teaches them coping strategies but also normalizes the process of dealing with difficult emotions.

Implement Structured Routines. Predictable routines can create a sense of security and stability for children with PTSD. Knowing what to expect throughout the day helps reduce anxiety and provides a framework within which they can express and manage their emotions. Create a daily schedule that includes regular times for meals, schoolwork, play, and relaxation. Consistency helps children feel safe and supports their emotional regulation.

Promote Positive Self-Talk. Encourage your child to use positive self-talk to counter negative or self-critical thoughts. Show them how to shift negative thoughts into positive affirmations. For example, if they're feeling anxious about a new situation, help them come up with reassuring statements like, "I am brave," or "I can handle this." Positive self-talk can improve self-esteem and help children feel more confident in their ability to manage their emotions.

Provide Opportunities for Physical Activity. Exercise is a great way for children to let go of excess energy and relieve stress. Activities like running, jumping, or playing sports can help regulate emotions and improve mood. Encourage your child to engage in activities they enjoy and find ways to incorporate movement into their daily routine. Physical activity not only supports emotional regulation but also contributes to overall physical health.

Support Social Connections. Building and maintaining positive relationships with peers can greatly benefit emotional regulation. Encourage your child to spend time with friends and participate in social activities that they enjoy. Positive social interactions provide opportunities for emotional expression and help children feel connected and supported.

Foster Creative Outlets. Creative activities such as art, music, or dance offer children alternative ways to express their emotions. Encourage your child to explore different forms of creativity and find what resonates with them. Creative outlets can be particularly helpful for children who find it difficult to verbalize their feelings, allowing them to channel their emotions into their artwork or performances.

By implementing these techniques, you can support your child in developing the skills they need to regulate and express their emotions effectively. It's important to remember that emotional regulation is a process that takes time and practice. Be patient and consistent in your support, and celebrate the progress your child makes along the way. Your encouragement and involvement play a key role in helping them build resilience and navigate their emotions with greater ease.

Mindfulness practices and relaxation exercises

Mindfulness practices and relaxation exercises are valuable tools for helping children with PTSD manage their emotions and reduce stress. By incorporating these techniques into daily routines, you can support your child in developing greater emotional awareness and self-regulation. Here's a detailed look at how mindfulness and relaxation practices can be beneficial and some practical ways to integrate them into your child's life. Mindfulness practices involve focusing on the present moment and accepting it without judgment. This can help children become more aware of their thoughts and feelings and learn to respond to them in a calm and controlled manner. Mindfulness exercises can be especially effective for children with PTSD as they promote a sense of calm and help manage overwhelming emotions.

One simple mindfulness practice is guided imagery. This involves leading your child through a calming mental exercise where they imagine a peaceful and safe place. For example, you might guide them to picture themselves sitting by a calm lake or in a cozy room. Encourage them to use all their senses to build a detailed mental image, such as feeling the warmth of the sun or hearing the gentle sounds of nature. Guided imagery helps your child relax and can be a comforting tool when they are feeling anxious or distressed.

Another effective mindfulness technique is body scan meditation. This exercise helps children become aware of physical sensations and release tension from their bodies. To practice a body scan, have your child lie down comfortably and close their eyes. Guide them through focusing on different parts of their body, starting from their toes and working up to their head. Encourage them to notice any areas of tension or discomfort and imagine letting go of that tension with each breath. This practice can help your child develop a greater connection to their body and promote relaxation.

Incorporating relaxation exercises into your child's routine can further support emotional regulation. Progressive muscle relaxation is a technique where your child tenses and then relaxes different muscle groups in their body. This practice helps them become more aware of physical tension and learn to release it. To start, have your child sit or lie down in a comfortable position. Guide them through tensing each muscle group for a few seconds and then releasing the tension. Begin with the muscles in their feet and work up to their head, focusing on one muscle group at a time. This exercise can be especially useful during times of high stress or anxiety.

Breathing exercises are another effective relaxation technique. Teach your child different breathing patterns, such as deep belly breathing or slow, rhythmic breathing. For deep belly breathing, have your child place one hand on their stomach and the other on their chest. Encourage them to take slow, deep breaths through their nose, allowing their stomach to rise and fall with each breath. This type of breathing helps engage the body's relaxation response and can reduce feelings of anxiety. Encouraging your child to practice mindfulness and relaxation exercises regularly can help them build resilience and improve their ability to manage stress. You can incorporate these practices into daily routines by setting aside specific times for mindfulness activities, such as before bedtime or after school. Make these practices engaging and enjoyable by using guided meditations or relaxation apps designed for children.

Creating a calm and supportive environment for mindfulness and relaxation is also important. Designate a quiet space in your home where your child can practice these techniques without distractions. This space should be comfortable and inviting, with soothing elements such as soft lighting or calming music. Encourage your child to use this space whenever they need a break or feel overwhelmed.

By integrating mindfulness practices and relaxation exercises into your child's routine, you can help them develop valuable skills for managing their emotions and reducing stress. These techniques offer practical ways for your child to cope with the challenges of PTSD and build a sense of calm and control in their daily life. With consistent practice and support, your child can learn to navigate their emotions with greater ease and confidence.

Ways to help children cope with anxiety and stress

Helping children cope with anxiety and stress involves providing them with practical tools and strategies that they can use to manage their emotions and navigate challenging situations. By equipping your child with effective coping mechanisms, you can support them in building resilience and finding a sense of calm. Here's a comprehensive look at various approaches to help children deal with anxiety and stress.

One of the most effective ways to help children cope with anxiety is by encouraging them to express their feelings. Creating a safe and open environment where your child feels comfortable sharing their thoughts and concerns is crucial. You can start by having regular conversations about their feelings and validating their experiences. For instance, if your child expresses worry about a specific event, acknowledge their feelings and reassure them that it's okay to be anxious. Encourage them to talk about what's making them feel this way and explore possible solutions together.

In addition to verbal expression, creative outlets such as drawing or writing can help children process their emotions. Providing your child with art supplies or a journal gives them a way to express their feelings visually or through writing. For example, they might draw a picture of what's causing their anxiety or write a story about their fears. Creative expression allows children to externalize their emotions and can be a therapeutic way to manage stress.

Teaching your child problem-solving skills can also help them handle anxiety and stress more effectively. Work with your child to identify the problem that is causing their stress and brainstorm possible solutions. Guide them in evaluating the pros and cons of each solution and help them choose a course of action. For instance, if your child is anxious about a school project, help them break the project into smaller, manageable tasks and create a plan for completing each one. By developing problem-solving skills, your child can feel more empowered and in control of their situation.

Another effective strategy is to introduce relaxation techniques that can be used in moments of heightened stress. Techniques such as deep breathing, progressive muscle relaxation, or visualization exercises can help your child calm their mind and body. Practice these techniques with your child regularly so they become familiar with them and know how to use them when needed. For example, during stressful situations, guide your child through deep breathing exercises by having them take slow, deep breaths and focus on their breathing to help reduce anxiety.

Establishing a consistent routine can also provide a sense of stability and predictability, which can be reassuring for children experiencing anxiety. A well-structured daily schedule helps children know what to expect and can reduce feelings of uncertainty. Include regular activities such as meal times, schoolwork, playtime, and relaxation periods in their routine. Consistency in daily activities helps create a secure environment where children feel more in control and less anxious.

Encouraging healthy lifestyle habits plays a significant role in managing anxiety and stress. Ensure your child gets regular physical activity, as exercise is known to reduce stress and improve mood. Activities like running, swimming, or playing a sport can be enjoyable ways for your child to release pent-up energy and boost their overall well-being. Additionally, maintain a balanced diet with nutritious foods and ensure your child gets enough sleep each night. Good sleep hygiene and a healthy diet contribute to emotional stability and resilience.

It's also important to model healthy coping strategies for your child. Children often learn by observing their parents, so demonstrating positive ways to handle stress can be beneficial. Share with your child how you manage your own stress and provide them with examples of effective coping techniques. For instance, if you're feeling stressed about work, show your child how you use relaxation exercises or take breaks to manage your emotions.

Finally, when anxiety and stress become overwhelming or persistent, seeking professional help may be necessary. A mental health professional can provide additional support and guidance tailored to your child's needs. Therapy can offer your child a safe space to explore their feelings and learn new coping strategies. If you notice that your child's anxiety is interfering with their daily life or causing significant distress, consider consulting a therapist or counselor who specializes in childhood anxiety and trauma.

By incorporating these strategies into your child's life, you can help them develop effective ways to cope with anxiety and stress. Providing support, encouragement, and practical tools empowers your child to manage their emotions and navigate challenging situations with greater confidence and resilience.

Tools and strategies for managing emotional outbursts

Managing emotional outbursts in children with PTSD requires a thoughtful approach that addresses both the immediate situation and the underlying causes of the outbursts. Emotional outbursts can be distressing for both the child and the parent, but with the right tools and strategies, you can help your child navigate these moments more effectively. Here's a detailed look at how to manage emotional outbursts and support your child in developing better emotional regulation skills.

One effective strategy for managing emotional outbursts is to remain calm and composed during the episode. Children often look to their parents for cues on how to react, so maintaining a steady demeanor can help de-escalate the situation. Take deep breaths, speak in a soothing voice, and avoid reacting with frustration or anger. By staying calm, you model emotional regulation for your child and create a more stable environment during their outburst.

Another helpful approach is to use distraction techniques to redirect your child's attention away from what's triggering their outburst. Gentle distractions can help shift their focus and provide a break from their intense emotions. For example, offer a favorite toy, suggest a different activity, or guide them to a calming space in the home. Distraction can give your child a moment to regroup and reduce the intensity of their emotional response.

Teaching and reinforcing coping skills is crucial for helping your child manage emotional outbursts. Work with your child to identify coping strategies that they can use when they feel overwhelmed. Techniques such as deep breathing, counting to ten, or using a calming phrase can be effective in managing strong emotions. Practice these techniques together regularly so your child becomes familiar with them and can use them during outbursts. For example, when your child starts to feel overwhelmed, remind them to take deep breaths and count slowly to help regain control.

Creating a **"calm-down"** corner or a designated space in the home where your child can go to calm down can be an effective tool. This space should be comfortable and soothing, with items like soft pillows, calming music, or sensory toys. Encourage your child to use this space when they feel an outburst coming on, allowing them to have a safe place to process their emotions and regain composure.

Setting clear and consistent expectations and boundaries is essential in managing emotional outbursts. Let your child know what behaviors are acceptable and what is not, and ensure that consequences for inappropriate behavior are consistently enforced. Consistency helps children understand the limits and expectations, reducing the likelihood of outbursts. For example, if your child understands that yelling and throwing objects are not acceptable, they are more likely to seek alternative ways to express their emotions.

It's also important to address the underlying causes of emotional outbursts by identifying and managing triggers. Observe patterns in your child's behavior to understand what might be causing their outbursts. Triggers can include specific situations, changes in routine, or unresolved stress. Once you identify these triggers, work with your child to develop strategies to manage or avoid them. For instance, if transitions between activities are a trigger, prepare your child in advance and provide reassurance during these times.

Building a strong emotional connection with your child can also help in managing outbursts. Spend quality time together, engage in positive interactions, and show empathy towards their feelings. A strong bond helps your child feel secure and understood, which can reduce the frequency and intensity of emotional outbursts. Regularly check in with your child about their feelings and let them know that you are there to support them.

In some cases, seeking professional help may be necessary if emotional outbursts are severe or persistent. A mental health professional can work with your child to address their emotional regulation challenges and provide additional strategies and support. Therapy can help your child develop coping skills and explore underlying issues contributing to their outbursts.

By employing these tools and strategies, you can help your child manage emotional outbursts more effectively. Remaining calm, using distraction, teaching coping skills, and addressing triggers are key components of supporting your child in navigating their emotions. Through consistent practice and support, your child can develop better emotional regulation skills and improve their overall well-being.

Chapter 6
Working with Professionals

When it comes to helping your child with PTSD, finding the right therapist or counselor is one of the most important steps. I know I've talked about seeking help back in Chapter 2, where we touched on making appointments and finding a therapist, but this topic is so crucial that it deserves an in-depth look here. A therapist or counselor plays a vital role in your child's healing journey, and the process of finding the right one can feel overwhelming. But with the right guidance, it's possible to make a choice that will help your child feel supported and understood.

The first thing to consider when selecting a therapist is the specific needs of your child. Not all therapists specialize in trauma or PTSD, so you'll want to look for someone who has experience in these areas. Ask about their background working with children, specifically those who have experienced trauma. A therapist trained in trauma-informed care will have the skills and sensitivity needed to handle your child's emotions in a safe and supportive way. This kind of approach helps children feel comfortable and less anxious about therapy, knowing that the person they're working with understands their situation on a deeper level.

Another important aspect is finding a therapist who makes both you and your child feel comfortable. While credentials and experience are key, the therapist's ability to connect with your child is equally important. Your child needs to trust and feel safe with the person who will be guiding them through difficult emotions. It may take a few sessions to determine if the therapist is a good fit, so don't hesitate to move on if something doesn't feel right. It's perfectly okay to trust your instincts as a parent in this process. You know your child best, and you'll be able to sense if the therapist is someone they can build a healthy relationship with.

Once you've narrowed down your list of potential therapists, it's time to ask questions. When reaching out to a therapist, ask about their experience with PTSD and what methods they use in treatment. Trauma-focused cognitive behavioral therapy (TF-CBT) is one of the most effective treatments for children with PTSD, and a therapist who is trained in this technique can be very beneficial for your child. You might also ask about play therapy or other creative approaches that can help your child express their feelings in a non-threatening way. Knowing how a therapist plans to approach treatment can help you feel more confident in your choice.

Cost is another factor to consider when selecting a therapist. Therapy can be expensive, but there are options that can make it more affordable. Check with your insurance provider to see what mental health services are covered, or look into sliding scale fees, which adjust based on your income. Some community clinics offer low-cost or free therapy services for children, especially those who have experienced trauma. Don't let financial concerns prevent you from seeking the help your child needs—there are often solutions available that can make therapy more accessible.

It's also a good idea to involve your child in the process when possible. Depending on their age and comfort level, you can explain to them what therapy is and why it's important. Let them know that the therapist is someone who will listen and help them understand their feelings better. Involving your child in the process of choosing a therapist can help them feel more in control and less apprehensive about starting therapy.

Finally, remember that finding the right therapist might take time. It's okay if the first person you meet with isn't the best fit for your child. The goal is to find someone who understands your child's unique needs and can offer the right kind of support. Patience and persistence are key in this process, and once you find the right therapist, the positive impact on your child's healing journey will be worth the effort.

Types of therapy and their benefits
(e.g., cognitive-behavioral therapy, play therapy)

There are different types of therapy that can help children with PTSD, each offering unique benefits depending on the child's needs and experiences. Understanding these types can help you make an informed decision when selecting the right therapeutic approach for your child. It's important to note that what works for one child may not necessarily work for another, so being open to various methods is essential in the healing process.

One of the most widely recognized and effective therapies for PTSD in children is Cognitive-Behavioral Therapy (CBT). Specifically, trauma-focused CBT (TF-CBT) has been shown to significantly reduce symptoms of PTSD. TF-CBT helps children process their traumatic experiences by encouraging them to talk about their feelings and thoughts related to the trauma. Through structured sessions, the therapist helps the child reframe their negative thoughts and develop healthier ways to cope with their emotions. TF-CBT also includes parental involvement, which allows you to support your child's progress and learn strategies to help them at home.

Another beneficial type of therapy is play therapy. This is especially effective for younger children who may not have the verbal skills to express what they're feeling. Play therapy uses toys, games, and creative activities to help children express themselves in a non-verbal way. Through play, children can communicate feelings they may not fully understand or be able to articulate. A trained play therapist observes the child's behavior during play and uses it to gain insight into the child's emotional state. This form of therapy can be incredibly powerful for children who struggle with trust or verbal communication after trauma, as it provides a safe space for them to process their emotions at their own pace.

Art therapy is another creative approach that can be beneficial for children with PTSD. Similar to play therapy, art therapy allows children to express their feelings through drawing, painting, or sculpting. For children who find it difficult to talk about their trauma, creating art can be a way to release pent-up emotions and explore their feelings in a safe, supportive environment. The act of creating something can also help children feel more in control, which is important for those who have experienced trauma and may feel a loss of control over their lives.

Eye Movement Desensitization and Reprocessing (EMDR) is another type of therapy that has been used effectively with children who have PTSD. EMDR focuses on helping the brain reprocess traumatic memories in a way that makes them less distressing. During an EMDR session, the therapist guides the child through a series of eye movements while they recall their traumatic experiences. This helps the brain to "digest" the trauma and reduce the emotional charge associated with it. Although this method may seem unconventional, many children and adults have found significant relief from PTSD symptoms after undergoing EMDR therapy.

Group therapy can also be helpful, particularly for older children and teens. In group therapy, children with similar experiences come together to share their feelings and support one another. For kids who feel isolated in their trauma, group therapy provides a sense of community and validation. Being able to connect with others who have been through similar situations can help reduce feelings of shame and help children see that they are not alone in their struggles. Group therapy can also teach valuable social skills and provide a safe space for children to practice expressing their emotions in front of others. Each of these therapeutic approaches offers distinct benefits, and sometimes a combination of therapies works best for a child. It's important to work closely with your child's therapist to find the right approach and to be patient as your child goes through the healing process. Therapy is a journey, and while the road may be long, each step brings your child closer to emotional healing and stability.

How to collaborate effectively with mental health professionals

Working closely with mental health professionals is a vital part of supporting your child through their healing journey. Effective collaboration between parents and therapists can make a big difference in the progress and overall well-being of a child with PTSD. The more open and cooperative this relationship is, the better the results tend to be for your child's recovery. Here are some important ways to collaborate effectively with mental health professionals.

The first key to successful collaboration is clear communication. Make sure you're consistently sharing updates with your child's therapist about changes in their behavior, emotions, and daily life. It's also important to bring up any concerns or questions you might have about the treatment. Sometimes, what your child tells the therapist in their sessions can differ from what you see at home, so maintaining a flow of information will help the therapist get a complete picture of how your child is doing. Don't be afraid to share small details, as these can often be valuable clues for the therapist in understanding what your child is going through.

Another important aspect is attending all recommended meetings and appointments. While life can get busy, making therapy sessions a priority shows your child that their mental health is important. Consistent involvement in the process also strengthens the partnership between you and the therapist. Whether it's a weekly session or a check-in to discuss your child's progress, your participation matters. If there's ever a conflict with your schedule, communicate this early with the therapist to reschedule, ensuring that your child's treatment remains uninterrupted.

Listening to the therapist's feedback and being open to their suggestions is also essential. Sometimes, the therapist may recommend changes in the home environment, or they may provide techniques for managing specific behaviors. Even if some of these suggestions seem unfamiliar or challenging at first, it's important to approach them with an open mind. Therapists are trained to understand the complexities of trauma, and their strategies are designed with your child's best interest in mind. Implementing their advice at home can significantly reinforce what your child is learning in therapy, creating a more cohesive healing experience.

Additionally, it's important to be patient with the process. Trauma recovery takes time, and progress may not always be immediate. Sometimes it can feel frustrating when your child seems to be moving slowly through therapy or if setbacks occur. However, staying supportive and encouraging through the ups and downs is crucial. Regularly discussing your child's progress with the therapist will help you understand what to expect and how to best support your child during this time.

Building a relationship of trust with the therapist is also important for effective collaboration. Just as your child needs to feel safe with their therapist, so do you. If at any point you feel unsure about the direction of the therapy or the approach being taken, don't hesitate to bring this up respectfully. A good therapist will welcome your input and work with you to find solutions that fit both your comfort level and your child's needs. Mutual respect and understanding between you and the therapist are the foundation for successful collaboration.

Lastly, don't forget to take care of yourself. Supporting a child through PTSD can be emotionally draining, and maintaining your own mental health is important. If you're feeling overwhelmed, consider seeking out your own support through counseling or parent support groups. This can provide you with helpful coping tools and make it easier to collaborate with your child's therapist from a place of emotional strength. Effective collaboration with mental health professionals is not just about attending sessions; it's about being an active, supportive partner in your child's journey to healing. By maintaining open communication, attending appointments, listening to the therapist's advice, and practicing patience, you can help create a strong, supportive team dedicated to your child's well-being.

Understanding therapy goals and progress

Understanding the goals of therapy and tracking progress are essential parts of your child's healing journey. Therapy is more than just attending sessions; it involves setting clear objectives and regularly evaluating how far your child has come. As a parent, knowing what these goals are and how progress is measured helps you stay involved and supportive in a meaningful way. Here's how you can better understand the purpose of therapy and how to gauge your child's development.

When therapy begins, the therapist typically outlines specific goals for your child. These goals are based on the unique challenges your child is facing and the type of trauma they've experienced. Goals might include improving emotional regulation, reducing anxiety, or building stronger coping mechanisms. It's important to take time to understand these goals because they serve as a roadmap for your child's recovery. Sometimes the therapist will break down larger goals into smaller, more manageable steps, helping your child work through their trauma at a pace that feels safe and achievable.

As therapy progresses, the therapist will assess how well your child is meeting these objectives. Progress can look different for every child. For some, it may be small changes like expressing their emotions more openly, while for others, it could be larger shifts like lessening the frequency of nightmares or anxiety attacks. What's important to remember is that progress isn't always linear. There might be periods of rapid improvement followed by moments where things seem to slow down or even regress. This is normal in trauma recovery, and it doesn't mean the therapy isn't working.

To stay informed about your child's progress, regular communication with the therapist is key. Therapists often use assessments or check-ins to determine how well the therapy is working. During these times, they might share insights into what's going well and where adjustments might be needed. It's essential to listen closely and ask questions when something isn't clear. If your child is comfortable, you might also encourage them to talk about how they feel therapy is helping them. Children may not always express it directly, but their emotions and behaviors can provide clues to how well they're responding to treatment.

You might also notice changes in your child's behavior at home, school, or during social interactions that indicate progress. Improved mood, fewer emotional outbursts, or more effective communication can all be signs that therapy is making a difference. However, it's important not to rely solely on these visible signs. Emotional healing can happen quietly and internally, so be patient and trust the process, even if it feels like things aren't changing as quickly as you'd hoped.

Therapy goals can also evolve over time. As your child achieves certain milestones, the therapist may adjust the treatment plan to focus on new challenges or deeper layers of trauma. This flexibility is essential, as it ensures the therapy remains responsive to your child's needs. Being involved in these goal-setting conversations allows you to provide valuable input and ensure that the direction of the therapy aligns with what's best for your child.

Another important part of understanding progress is celebrating achievements, no matter how small. Each step your child takes in therapy is a step toward healing, and acknowledging their hard work can boost their confidence and motivation. Whether it's completing a difficult exercise, opening up about their feelings, or using a coping strategy during a stressful moment, these victories matter. By recognizing and celebrating them, you show your child that you see their effort and that their progress is meaningful.

Lastly, don't be discouraged by setbacks. Trauma recovery is often a long, winding road, and setbacks are a natural part of the process. If your child experiences a regression or struggles with a particular aspect of therapy, it's not a sign of failure. Instead, view it as an opportunity to revisit goals and explore different approaches. Sometimes, setbacks can reveal deeper emotional issues that need to be addressed, leading to even more meaningful breakthroughs later on.

Understanding therapy goals and progress is a collaborative effort between you, your child, and the therapist. By staying informed, being patient, and celebrating every step forward, you can help your child navigate their path to healing with confidence and resilience.

Managing and monitoring the therapeutic process

Managing and monitoring the therapeutic process is a crucial part of supporting your child through trauma recovery. Therapy isn't just about attending appointments and hoping for the best. As a parent, your active involvement in overseeing the process can make a significant difference in how effective the treatment is for your child. While therapists bring professional expertise, your understanding and input are invaluable in ensuring your child's needs are being met.

One of the first steps in managing the therapeutic process is establishing clear lines of communication with the therapist. From the outset, you'll want to maintain regular updates on how things are going. This doesn't mean you need to be involved in every detail of your child's sessions—especially if privacy is essential for their comfort—but rather that you have a good understanding of the overall direction of the therapy. Knowing what specific goals the therapist is working toward with your child, and how they are measuring success, gives you a sense of how things are progressing. If the therapist is comfortable sharing insights, it's helpful to ask questions about the process and inquire about areas where you can support your child at home.

At home, you can monitor your child's emotional and behavioral changes. Pay close attention to how they respond to stress, how they handle conflicts, and how they manage daily tasks that might have previously been overwhelming. You're in a unique position to observe how the tools and strategies your child learns in therapy translate to everyday life. If you notice positive changes, like increased emotional regulation or reduced anxiety, it's a sign that the therapy is having a beneficial impact. On the other hand, if you observe ongoing or new struggles, it may be time to talk to the therapist about adjusting the approach.

Flexibility is key in managing the therapeutic process. Trauma recovery doesn't follow a predictable path, so the treatment plan might need adjustments along the way. This could involve shifting focus to different therapy techniques, revisiting certain goals, or even changing the frequency of sessions. Stay open to these changes and trust that they are part of your child's healing journey. Working with the therapist to periodically review and adjust the plan ensures that your child continues to receive the support they need.

If you feel that your child's therapy isn't moving in the right direction or that progress has stalled, it's important to address these concerns early. Therapy can sometimes reach plateaus, and that's perfectly normal. However, if you're worried that your child isn't benefiting as much as they could be, talk to the therapist about your concerns. There might be underlying issues affecting the therapy's effectiveness, or perhaps your child's needs have evolved and require a new strategy. The key is to maintain open, non-confrontational communication so that the focus remains on your child's well-being.

Another important aspect of managing the therapeutic process is keeping track of logistical details like appointments, insurance, and costs. While these may seem secondary to the emotional aspects of therapy, managing them smoothly can reduce stress for both you and your child. Staying organized ensures that your child doesn't miss appointments and that their therapy remains consistent, which is vital for maintaining progress. If financial concerns arise, don't hesitate to ask about alternative options, sliding scale fees, or other forms of support that may be available.

It's also crucial to monitor how your child feels about the therapy itself. While they may not always express it directly, paying attention to their mood before and after sessions can provide valuable insight. Some children may feel anxious or resistant about therapy at first, which is natural, but over time they should begin to feel more comfortable and secure with the process. If your child consistently shows signs of distress, it may be worth exploring with the therapist whether the current approach is the right fit. Your child's emotional safety and comfort should always be at the forefront of any therapeutic work.

Lastly, as a parent, it's important to maintain your own well-being while managing your child's therapy. Supporting a child through trauma can be emotionally draining, and it's easy to feel overwhelmed at times. Seeking your own support, whether through a counselor, support group, or trusted friends and family, can help you stay grounded. Remember, you're not just a caretaker; you're also a partner in your child's healing journey, and taking care of yourself ensures you can continue to provide the support your child needs.

Managing and monitoring the therapeutic process requires patience, communication, and flexibility. By staying actively involved, ensuring open dialogue with the therapist, and being attuned to your child's emotional needs, you create a solid foundation for their ongoing recovery. Your role is to provide both structure and comfort as your child navigates the complexities of trauma healing, and together with the therapist, you can help them build the tools they need for long-term emotional well-being.

Chapter 7
Self-Care for Parents

When you're parenting a child with PTSD, it's easy to become so focused on your child's needs that you forget to care for yourself. Stress can build up, leaving you feeling overwhelmed, emotionally drained, and physically exhausted. It's important to remember that you can't pour from an empty cup. Your well-being matters just as much as your child's, and maintaining your own emotional health is key to being the best support for them. Learning how to manage stress and maintain emotional balance is an essential part of this journey.

One of the most practical strategies for managing stress as a parent is learning how to recognize the early signs. Stress doesn't always hit all at once—it often creeps in slowly, manifesting in physical, emotional, or behavioral ways. You may start feeling unusually tired, more irritable than usual, or even withdrawn from activities you normally enjoy. By staying mindful of these signals, you can take steps to address stress before it reaches overwhelming levels. This could mean taking a few moments to pause and breathe deeply when you notice tension rising, or acknowledging that it's okay to need a break sometimes.

Creating small routines for self-care throughout your day is another important way to manage stress. They don't need to be complicated or take much time. Even a short walk in the morning, a few moments of silence before bed, or enjoying a warm cup of tea in the afternoon can help ground you and provide mental clarity. Consistency in these small acts of self-care sends a message to yourself that your needs are important, and it can provide a buffer against the relentless pressures of caregiving.

Another helpful strategy for managing stress is to set realistic expectations for yourself. Parenting a child with PTSD comes with its own set of unique challenges, and it's important to accept that not every day will go smoothly. It's easy to feel guilty when things don't go as planned or when you don't meet the high standards you've set for yourself. However, learning to show yourself the same grace and compassion that you offer your child is essential. Let go of the idea of perfection and focus on progress instead. Celebrate the small victories, even if it's just making it through a tough day with your patience intact.

Finding time to connect with others is also crucial for maintaining emotional health. When you're deep in the day-to-day of managing your child's trauma, it's easy to feel isolated, like no one else understands what you're going through. But reaching out to a support network, whether that's close friends, family, or a community of other parents facing similar challenges, can provide comfort. Sharing your experiences, venting frustrations, or simply hearing a kind word from someone who understands can make a world of difference. It's not just about getting advice—it's about feeling seen and supported.

Physical exercise, even in small amounts, is another proven way to reduce stress and improve your mood. Exercise releases endorphins, the body's natural stress relievers, and helps combat feelings of fatigue or sluggishness that often come with chronic stress. You don't have to commit to a rigorous workout routine—something as simple as stretching, walking, or dancing to your favorite music can be incredibly beneficial. The goal is to move your body in a way that feels good to you, helping you release pent-up tension and clear your mind.

Journaling is another tool that can help you process your emotions. Writing down your thoughts and feelings allows you to reflect on the challenges you're facing without judgment. It can also serve as a release, giving you a safe space to express frustrations, fears, and hopes. By putting your thoughts on paper, you might find clarity on issues that felt too overwhelming to tackle in the moment. It can also be a great way to track your progress, noticing how far you've come and acknowledging the growth you've experienced as both a parent and a person.

Lastly, it's important to set boundaries when it comes to managing your time and energy. As much as you want to give your all to your child, it's not sustainable to neglect your own needs for too long. Saying no to additional commitments, asking for help when you need it, and prioritizing time for yourself aren't selfish acts—they are essential for maintaining your health. Knowing your limits and respecting them ensures that you can continue to show up for your child in the most loving and supportive way possible.

Taking care of your emotional health is an ongoing process. Just as your child's recovery from trauma will have ups and downs, so will your own journey toward finding balance and managing stress. Be kind to yourself, and remember that your well-being is deeply connected to your ability to care for your child. By making your self-care a priority, you're not only nurturing yourself but also modeling healthy emotional regulation for your child.

Importance of setting boundaries and finding balance

As a parent of a child with PTSD, setting boundaries and finding balance is crucial for both your emotional health and your child's well-being. It's easy to become consumed with your child's needs, but without boundaries, you risk burnout, frustration, and emotional exhaustion. The goal of boundaries isn't to shut out your child's needs but to create a healthier relationship where you can support them without losing yourself in the process. When you set clear limits on what you can handle, you are better equipped to show up for them in a meaningful and supportive way.

One of the most important aspects of setting boundaries is recognizing your personal limits. Parenting a child with PTSD can be demanding, but it's important to acknowledge that you have limits on your time, energy, and emotional reserves. Saying "no" when you feel overwhelmed, asking for help when you need it, or taking time for yourself are necessary acts of self-care. It's okay to tell your child that you need a break, or to ask your partner or a trusted family member to step in when you're feeling stretched too thin. When you honor your own needs, you are better able to meet your child's needs in the long run.

Boundaries also help in managing your expectations. It's essential to remember that you don't have to do everything or solve every problem. There will be times when you cannot fix your child's distress or heal their pain immediately, and that's okay. Accepting that your role is to provide support, not to be a miracle worker, can alleviate some of the pressure you may feel. Setting realistic expectations for yourself and your child is a form of boundary-setting that allows you to focus on what is possible and within your control, rather than feeling overwhelmed by what isn't.

Another aspect of boundary-setting is learning to say no to outside demands. Whether it's work, extended family, or other social obligations, it's important to recognize that your time and energy are not infinite. Taking on too much outside of your family life can lead to stress that detracts from your ability to be present for your child. It's okay to limit your involvement in activities that don't serve your emotional well-being. Giving yourself permission to prioritize what truly matters—your own health and your child's recovery—helps you maintain balance in your life.

Finding balance means making sure that your life includes time for things that nourish and restore you. This might look like carving out moments for hobbies, connecting with friends, or simply having quiet time to yourself. It's easy to feel guilty for taking time away from your child, but in reality, taking care of yourself makes you a better parent. Balance isn't just about equal time for yourself and your child; it's about ensuring that neither is neglected. Both your needs and your child's needs are important, and finding a rhythm that honors both is key.

Creating a sense of balance also involves teaching your child about boundaries. Kids, especially those with PTSD, can have difficulty understanding or accepting that their parents have needs, too. Explaining that everyone in the family has the right to their own space and time helps them understand that boundaries are not about rejection but about maintaining healthy relationships. You can model this by demonstrating how you take care of yourself, whether it's by stepping away for a moment of calm or saying no when necessary. This teaches your child that setting limits is not only acceptable but essential for emotional health.

Ultimately, boundaries and balance are about preserving your own well-being while creating a supportive environment for your child. By being clear about your own needs and teaching your child to respect them, you foster a home where everyone's emotional health is valued. This also helps prevent resentment from building, which can sometimes happen when a parent feels overwhelmed by caregiving responsibilities. By prioritizing balance and boundaries, you create a healthier, more sustainable dynamic where both you and your child can thrive.

Self-care routines and practices for parents

Self-care routines and practices are essential for parents, especially when caring for a child with PTSD. It's easy to put your own needs last when your child is struggling, but consistent self-care is not a luxury—it's a necessity. Taking time to nurture your own physical, emotional, and mental well-being helps you stay resilient, patient, and capable of providing the best care for your child. Without tending to your own health, it becomes increasingly difficult to manage the challenges that come with parenting a child who has experienced trauma.

The first aspect of building a self-care routine is recognizing what truly replenishes you. Self-care isn't a one-size-fits-all practice; it looks different for everyone. Some parents may find that physical activity, like a daily walk or a yoga session, helps release stress and restore energy. Others may benefit from creative outlets such as writing, painting, or even baking. The key is to identify what activities make you feel grounded and recharged, and then integrate those practices into your daily routine. Even just 10 to 15 minutes a day of intentional self-care can make a big difference in how you feel.

Mindfulness practices are another helpful self-care tool. Mindfulness is about being present in the moment without judgment, which can be incredibly grounding during stressful times. Simple techniques like deep breathing exercises, guided meditation, or even pausing to notice your surroundings can help calm your mind and body. These moments of mindfulness can serve as brief but powerful breaks in your day, allowing you to reset emotionally and mentally, which is especially helpful when the demands of parenting start to feel overwhelming.

One practice to incorporate is setting aside quiet time for reflection. Journaling is a great way to process your thoughts and emotions, especially when you're feeling overwhelmed by your child's needs or your own stress. Writing down what you're feeling can help you make sense of it, providing a sense of release and clarity. It can also help you track patterns, noticing when certain stressors are consistently affecting your mood, so you can address them more proactively. You might also use this time to reflect on positive moments or progress your child has made, which can remind you of the good amidst the challenging days.

Sleep is another vital component of self-care that is often overlooked by parents. Lack of sleep can make you feel more irritable, less patient, and less able to cope with stress. Establishing a regular sleep routine is crucial. Try to go to bed at the same time each night and create a calming bedtime ritual, such as reading or listening to soft music, to help signal to your brain that it's time to wind down. If falling or staying asleep is a struggle due to stress or worry, consider relaxation techniques like a warm bath before bed or listening to calming nature sounds. Prioritizing rest allows you to face each new day with more energy and clarity.

Nutrition also plays a significant role in self-care. When life gets busy and overwhelming, it's easy to turn to convenience foods that may not offer the best nutrition. However, eating well-balanced, nourishing meals fuels your body and mind, giving you the energy to manage the demands of parenting. Preparing simple, healthy meals in advance or keeping quick, nutritious snacks on hand can help you maintain steady energy throughout the day. Hydration is equally important; drinking enough water can help you avoid fatigue and keep your mind clear. The goal is to view eating as an act of self-care that helps you maintain the strength to care for your family.

Social support is another essential piece of self-care. Caring for a child with PTSD can feel isolating at times, so it's important to stay connected with others. Whether it's a close friend, family member, or a support group of other parents going through similar experiences, having people to talk to can be a lifeline. It's okay to ask for help or even just to vent when you're feeling frustrated or overwhelmed. Sometimes, simply knowing that someone else understands what you're going through can make all the difference. Make time for social interactions that bring you joy and laughter, as those moments of connection can significantly reduce stress.

Incorporating self-compassion into your routine is also important. As a parent, it's natural to feel guilt or self-doubt, wondering if you're doing enough or handling things the right way. Practicing self-compassion means being kind to yourself when things don't go perfectly. It's recognizing that parenting, especially in the context of trauma, is hard, and it's okay to have tough days. Talk to yourself the way you would comfort a friend—remind yourself that you're doing your best, and that's enough. This mindset shift can help you maintain emotional resilience, even on the toughest days.

Ultimately, self-care is about taking intentional steps to nurture your own well-being so you can be fully present for your child. When you establish routines that prioritize your physical, emotional, and mental health, you're not only benefiting yourself but also modeling for your child how important it is to take care of oneself. By showing them that self-care is a priority, you're teaching them lifelong skills for managing stress and maintaining balance in their own lives.

Seeking support and building a support network

Seeking support and building a strong support network are crucial components of self-care for parents, especially when managing the emotional and physical demands of raising a child with PTSD. No one is meant to face these challenges alone, and surrounding yourself with supportive people can make a significant difference in your well-being. The idea of asking for help can sometimes feel daunting, but it's important to remember that seeking support is not a sign of weakness. Instead, it's an essential part of caring for yourself and your family.

The first step in building a support network is recognizing who is available and willing to offer support. This could include close friends, family members, or even neighbors who understand your situation and are ready to help. When you reach out to others, be specific about your needs. Sometimes, people want to help but don't know how. For example, you might ask a friend to watch your child for an hour so you can take a break or run an errand. Or, you might ask a family member to lend an ear when you need to talk about your worries and frustrations. Clear communication about your needs makes it easier for others to step in and offer meaningful support.

Another valuable source of support is a parenting or caregiver support group. These groups bring together parents who are facing similar challenges, creating a space for shared understanding and empathy. In a support group, you can share your experiences, listen to others, and gain new perspectives on how to handle difficult situations. The benefit of these groups is that they provide a sense of community and reassurance that you're not alone. Hearing how other parents cope with similar struggles can provide comfort and even inspire new strategies you may not have considered. Many groups also offer a judgment-free zone where you can speak openly about your feelings, something that can be harder to do with people who don't fully understand your circumstances.

You can also seek professional support to bolster your network. A therapist or counselor can help you navigate the emotional toll that parenting a child with PTSD can take. They can provide tools and techniques for managing your stress, improving your communication with your child, and maintaining your emotional health. Regular sessions with a mental health professional can offer a dedicated space for you to reflect on your well-being, helping you gain insight into your own needs and challenges. Just as your child benefits from professional guidance, you can, too, by seeking out experts who specialize in caregiver or parental support.

Faith-based communities can also offer meaningful support for some parents. If spirituality or faith plays an important role in your life, connecting with others who share your beliefs can be a source of strength. Many churches, mosques, synagogues, or other religious institutions provide community outreach and support services that can include emotional support, counseling, or even practical assistance. Whether through prayer groups, pastoral counseling, or simply connecting with like-minded individuals, faith-based networks can provide a sense of hope and encouragement during difficult times.

In addition to emotional support, practical help can also come from building a broader network of professionals and community resources. This might include working with social workers, medical professionals, or community centers that offer services for families. These resources can help lighten the load by connecting you with services or programs that support both you and your child's needs. Sometimes, accessing these kinds of services can provide immediate relief, whether it's through financial assistance, respite care, or educational resources that help you better understand trauma and its impact on your family.

It's also important to recognize that seeking support is a continual process. Your needs may change over time, and that's okay. Don't be afraid to re-evaluate your support system periodically and make adjustments as needed. Some relationships may naturally grow stronger as you share more about your journey, while others may not be as involved. It's important to surround yourself with people who genuinely understand your situation and are willing to provide the kind of support that makes a real difference in your day-to-day life.

Ultimately, the goal of building a support network is to create a circle of people and resources that you can rely on in times of need. By accepting help from others, you're not only taking care of yourself but also ensuring that you have the emotional and practical capacity to care for your child. It's essential to remember that it's okay to lean on others—doing so strengthens your ability to be the best parent you can be, especially when facing the unique challenges of raising a child with PTSD.

Resources for parental well-being
(e.g., counseling, support groups)

Resources for parental well-being are vital for maintaining the emotional, mental, and physical health of parents, especially when they are supporting a child with PTSD. Parenting a child who has experienced trauma can be emotionally draining, and it's important to acknowledge that taking care of yourself is not a luxury, but a necessity. Fortunately, there are a variety of resources available that can help parents build resilience, find emotional support, and manage the stress that comes with this challenging role.

One of the most effective resources for parental well-being is counseling or therapy. Just as therapy can help children process their trauma, it can also be a powerful tool for parents. Engaging in individual therapy gives you a safe space to explore your feelings, cope with the demands of parenting a child with PTSD, and address any personal stress or emotional difficulties. Therapists who specialize in trauma, parental stress, or caregiver support can provide strategies to help you maintain your emotional balance while navigating the unique challenges your child's needs present. Additionally, many parents find that therapy helps them better understand their own emotional triggers and how to respond to their child's behavior in a more thoughtful, constructive way.

Support groups are another valuable resource for parents. In a support group, you can connect with other parents who are going through similar experiences, share stories, and learn from each other. These groups offer a sense of community and validation, as you realize that you are not alone in your journey. Hearing from others who are walking a similar path can bring comfort and insight. You might discover new strategies for managing your child's PTSD symptoms, hear about resources you hadn't considered, or simply feel encouraged by knowing that others understand what you are going through. Many support groups are facilitated by professionals who can guide discussions and offer expert advice, making them a practical and emotional lifeline for parents.

Another helpful resource is online communities and forums. For parents who may not have access to in-person support groups, or who prefer the flexibility of connecting with others from home, online communities provide a space to ask questions, share experiences, and receive support. Many websites and social media platforms host forums or groups specifically for parents of children with PTSD. These platforms can be a great way to seek advice, read about other families' coping mechanisms, and even participate in discussions about various treatment options or self-care techniques. However, it's important to engage in these spaces with discernment, focusing on well-moderated groups that offer constructive and respectful dialogue.

Faith-based counseling or spiritual support can also play a key role in parental well-being, especially for those who find strength in their faith or religious community. Many churches, synagogues, mosques, or other religious institutions offer counseling services, spiritual direction, or peer support for parents facing difficult circumstances. For some parents, prayer groups or pastoral counseling provide emotional support and a sense of peace during turbulent times. Spiritual resources often focus on finding hope, inner peace, and strength through faith, which can help parents sustain their emotional well-being when facing the everyday challenges of parenting a child with PTSD.

Additionally, educational resources such as books, webinars, or workshops focused on trauma-informed parenting can be incredibly useful. These resources often provide detailed insights into how trauma affects children, practical tips for managing difficult behaviors, and strategies for building a more peaceful home environment. By educating yourself, you not only empower your parenting but also gain confidence in knowing you are taking informed steps to support both your child and yourself. Workshops or parenting classes, especially those focused on trauma, can also offer opportunities for connecting with other parents while learning valuable skills.

Community-based organizations, such as nonprofits or local family support services, can also offer practical resources for parental well-being. Many communities have agencies that provide respite care, which allows parents to take breaks while trained professionals care for their children. These services can be a relief for parents who need time to recharge and focus on their own self-care. Additionally, community centers may offer wellness programs, family counseling services, or other resources designed to support families dealing with trauma.

Finally, self-help tools such as meditation apps, relaxation exercises, and self-care journals can also be beneficial. These tools help parents manage their stress and anxiety on a day-to-day basis, giving them small but effective ways to focus on their own well-being. Guided meditations, mindfulness exercises, and breathing techniques can be easily accessed through mobile apps, and they offer a convenient way to take a break and center yourself, even on busy days.

In conclusion, the well-being of parents is essential to the overall health of the family. By seeking out resources like therapy, support groups, educational materials, and community services, parents can build a strong foundation of emotional and practical support. Taking the time to care for your own mental and emotional health is one of the most important things you can do, not only for yourself but also for your child. In accessing these resources, you give yourself the strength and resilience needed to navigate the complexities of parenting a child with PTSD, and you model the importance of self-care for your entire family.

Chapter 8
Practical Strategies for Everyday Challenges

Handling specific issues like nightmares, flashbacks, and anxiety can be particularly challenging when parenting a child with PTSD. Each of these problems can significantly impact your child's daily life and your family's routine. However, there are practical strategies that can help address these issues effectively and compassionately.

Nightmares are a common issue for children with PTSD. They can cause distress, disrupt sleep, and create a fear of going to bed. One effective strategy for dealing with nightmares is establishing a calming bedtime routine. This routine should be predictable and soothing to help your child feel safe and secure before going to sleep. You might include activities such as reading a favorite book, listening to gentle music, or practicing relaxation exercises. Creating a comfortable and safe sleep environment is also crucial. Make sure your child's bedroom is a calming space, free from distractions and sources of anxiety. You might use soft lighting or a nightlight if darkness is a concern, and ensure their bedding is cozy and comforting.

Another approach is to help your child process their nightmares. Encourage them to talk about their dreams if they're comfortable doing so. Sometimes, expressing their fears can reduce their intensity. You can also help your child create a "dream catcher" or a similar comforting ritual that can symbolize their protection and safety. If nightmares persist and cause significant distress, it might be helpful to consult with a therapist who can offer specialized techniques for managing trauma-related sleep issues.

Flashbacks are another challenging issue for children with PTSD. They can be frightening and disorienting, causing your child to relive traumatic experiences. When a flashback occurs, it's important to stay calm and provide reassurance. Gently ground your child in the present moment by using techniques such as reminding them of their current surroundings, encouraging them to take deep breaths, or using sensory objects like a favorite toy or a comforting texture. Consistent grounding techniques can help your child feel more secure and less overwhelmed during a flashback.

Creating a **"flashback plan"** can also be helpful. Work with your child to develop a list of strategies they can use when they start to feel overwhelmed. This list might include breathing exercises, calming self-talk, or reaching out to a trusted adult. Practicing these techniques during calm moments can make them more effective when your child is experiencing a flashback. Anxiety is a common issue for children with PTSD and can manifest in various ways, such as excessive worry, restlessness, or physical symptoms like stomachaches. One effective way to manage anxiety is to teach your child relaxation techniques. Simple breathing exercises, progressive muscle relaxation, or guided imagery can help them manage their anxiety. Practice these techniques together so that your child feels confident using them when they are feeling anxious.

Building a predictable and supportive routine can also help reduce anxiety. Children with PTSD often feel more secure when they know what to expect. Establish regular schedules for meals, bedtime, and other daily activities to create a sense of stability. Consistent routines help children feel more in control and less anxious about the unknown.

In addition to these strategies, it's important to be mindful of your child's overall emotional and psychological needs. Promote honest conversations and create a secure environment for your child to share their emotions. Let them know that it's okay to talk about their worries and that they have your support. Being a reassuring and understanding presence can make a significant difference in how your child copes with anxiety.

If these issues persist or become overwhelming, seeking professional help is a valuable option. Therapists specializing in trauma and PTSD can offer additional strategies and support tailored to your child's specific needs. They can work with your child to develop coping mechanisms and provide guidance on how to manage symptoms more effectively.

Dealing with nightmares, flashbacks, and anxiety requires a combination of practical strategies and emotional support. By creating a safe and predictable environment, practicing calming techniques, and seeking professional help when needed, you can help your child manage these challenges and improve their overall well-being.

Strategies for dealing with school and social situations

Dealing with school and social situations can be particularly challenging for children with PTSD. They may struggle with anxiety, avoidance, or difficulty in social interactions, which can impact their overall experience and performance. Here's how you can support your child through these situations effectively: When it comes to school, it's important to communicate openly with teachers and school staff. Inform them about your child's PTSD and any specific challenges they might face. Schools often have resources and accommodations that can help your child succeed. For instance, you might work with the school to develop a personalized education plan or 504 plan that includes accommodations like extended time on tests, a quiet place for breaks, or flexible deadlines. This ensures that your child's educational needs are met and that they have a supportive environment in which they can thrive.

Encourage your child to establish a routine for school that includes both academic and social aspects. Consistent daily routines can help them feel more secure and reduce anxiety. This might involve setting up a structured morning routine, organizing school materials, and planning after-school activities. Routines provide a sense of predictability, which can be comforting for a child with PTSD.

For social situations, it's helpful to role-play different scenarios with your child. Practice how they might handle common social interactions, such as joining a group of friends, dealing with conflicts, or speaking up in class. Role-playing can build confidence and give your child strategies to manage these situations effectively. It's also important to teach them social skills and coping mechanisms, such as how to initiate conversations, maintain eye contact, or manage social anxiety.

Encourage your child to participate in social activities that interest them, but be mindful of their comfort level. Start with small, manageable activities and gradually increase their involvement as they become more comfortable. This might include joining a club, participating in a team sport, or attending social events. Providing support and encouragement while respecting their boundaries is key to helping them navigate social situations.

Building a strong support network within their social environment is also beneficial. Encourage your child to develop friendships with peers who are understanding and supportive. Positive relationships can provide emotional support and help them feel more connected and less isolated. If your child is struggling to make friends or navigate social interactions, consider involving a school counselor or therapist who can provide additional support and guidance.

In addition to these strategies, it's important to be patient and understanding of your child's needs. Social and school-related challenges can be overwhelming for children with PTSD, and they may need extra time and support to adjust. Provide comfort and acknowledge their achievements, no matter how minor. Positive reinforcement can boost their confidence and motivate them to continue working through their challenges.

If your child's difficulties in school or social situations persist or worsen, seeking professional help is advisable. Therapists who specialize in trauma and PTSD can offer targeted interventions to address these issues. They can work with your child to develop coping strategies, improve social skills, and manage anxiety related to school and social interactions.

Overall, supporting your child through school and social situations involves open communication, structured routines, and patience. By providing a supportive environment, practicing social skills, and seeking professional help when needed, you can help your child navigate these challenges and build a positive experience in both their educational and social environments.

Balancing discipline with support and understanding

Balancing discipline with support and understanding is crucial for helping children with PTSD navigate their behaviors while feeling secure and valued. Discipline is important for teaching boundaries and expectations, but it must be combined with empathy and support to be effective. Here's how to achieve this balance:

Start by setting clear, consistent rules and expectations. Children with PTSD benefit from having a structured environment where they understand what is expected of them. Clearly communicate the rules and the reasons behind them in a way that is easy for your child to understand. For example, instead of saying, **"You need to behave better,"** explain, **"We need to use indoor voices because it helps everyone stay focused and calm."** Consistency in enforcing rules helps create a sense of stability, which is important for children dealing with trauma.

When a rule is broken, address the behavior calmly and constructively. Focus on the specific behavior rather than labeling the child. For instance, instead of saying, **"You are being bad,"** you might say, **"Throwing your toys is not okay because it can hurt someone."** This approach helps your child understand what went wrong and how to correct it without feeling attacked or unworthy.

Provide choices and involve your child in problem-solving. Giving children with PTSD a sense of control can reduce their anxiety and help them feel more secure. When dealing with behavioral issues, offer choices that allow your child to make decisions within set boundaries. For example, if they're having trouble with homework, let them choose between working on it now or after a short break. This approach empowers them and encourages cooperation while still guiding them towards acceptable behavior.

Incorporate positive reinforcement to encourage desired behaviors. Notice and applaud your child's efforts and successes, no matter how minor. Positive reinforcement can be a powerful tool in helping children feel valued and motivated. For instance, if your child follows the rules or makes a positive choice, acknowledge it with specific praise, such as, **"I'm proud of how you used your indoor voice today. It really helped us stay calm."**

While discipline is important, it's equally crucial to provide emotional support. Understand that children with PTSD may have reactions that are linked to their trauma rather than intentional defiance. Approach their behaviors with empathy and try to understand the underlying emotions. For example, if your child becomes upset during a transition or change, recognize that it might be linked to their past experiences and not just a resistance to following rules.

Encourage open communication about feelings and behaviors. Create an environment where your child feels safe to express their emotions and concerns. Let them know that it's okay to talk about their feelings and that they will be heard and supported. This open dialogue helps your child feel understood and less isolated in their experiences.

Be flexible and willing to adapt your approach as needed. Each child's needs are different, and what works for one may not be effective for another. If a particular disciplinary strategy isn't effective, consider adjusting it or trying a different approach. Regularly assess how your strategies are working and be open to making changes that better meet your child's needs.

Lastly, maintain a focus on building a strong, trusting relationship with your child. A supportive relationship provides a foundation for effective discipline. When children feel loved and understood, they are more likely to respond positively to guidance and support. Invest time in connecting with your child through shared activities, open conversations, and expressions of affection.

Balancing discipline with support and understanding involves setting clear expectations, addressing behavior calmly, providing choices, reinforcing positive actions, and offering emotional support. By combining these elements, you create an environment where your child feels secure, valued, and motivated to grow and learn.

Practical tips for managing daily routines and interactions

Managing daily routines and interactions effectively is key to creating a stable environment for children with PTSD. Establishing a structured daily routine and mindful interactions can greatly help in reducing anxiety and providing a sense of security. Here's how to make daily routines and interactions as smooth and supportive as possible:

Create a Consistent Routine: Children with PTSD thrive on routine as it provides a sense of predictability and control. Establish daily routines for waking up, meals, school, and bedtime. Try to stick to these routines as closely as possible, even on weekends or during holidays, to maintain stability. Consistent routines help children know what to expect and can reduce anxiety about the unknown.

Use Visual Schedules: Visual schedules can be a helpful tool for children with PTSD, as they offer a clear and tangible way to understand what will happen throughout the day. Create a visual schedule using pictures or icons that represent different activities. Place the schedule where your child can easily see it, and review it together each morning to help them prepare for the day ahead.

Incorporate Transitions Smoothly: Transitions between activities can be challenging for children with PTSD. To ease transitions, provide warnings before changing activities. For example, you might use a timer or give a five-minute warning before moving from playtime to mealtime. This approach helps your child prepare for the change and reduces stress associated with sudden shifts.

Maintain a Calm Environment: Aim to keep the environment calm and orderly, as this can help your child feel more secure. Avoid loud noises or chaotic situations that might overwhelm them. Create a calming space where your child can go to relax if they start to feel overwhelmed. This could be a quiet corner with comforting items like soft pillows or a favorite book.

Encourage Positive Interactions: Positive interactions and encouragement are important for building trust and confidence. Make an effort to recognize and praise your child's efforts and achievements. Simple affirmations and positive reinforcement help build their self-esteem and reinforce good behavior. For instance, acknowledging their effort in completing a task or handling a situation well can encourage them to continue making positive choices.

Promote Healthy Communication: Foster open communication by encouraging your child to express their feelings and thoughts. Listen actively and validate their emotions, showing that you understand and care about what they are experiencing. Use simple and clear language to discuss daily activities and any changes in routine. This helps your child feel heard and supported.

Set Clear Expectations and Boundaries: Clearly outline expectations for behavior and routines, and be consistent in enforcing them. Children with PTSD benefit from understanding the rules and the reasons behind them. For example, explain why it's important to follow certain routines or rules and what the consequences will be if they are not followed. Provide Choices Where Possible: Giving your child choices can help them feel more in control and reduce resistance to routines. Offer options within structured routines, such as choosing between two activities or selecting a snack from a few healthy options. This empowers your child and can make daily routines feel more manageable.

Incorporate Relaxation Techniques: Integrate relaxation techniques into your daily routine to help manage stress and anxiety. Simple practices like deep breathing exercises, stretching, or short mindfulness activities can be calming for children with PTSD. Make these practices a regular part of the day, especially during transitions or challenging moments.

Be Patient and Flexible: Understand that routines may need to be adjusted based on your child's needs and mood. Flexibility is important, as rigid adherence to routines may not always be practical. Be patient with your child and willing to adapt routines as needed to better support their well-being.

Encourage Independence: While maintaining a structured routine, encourage your child to take on age-appropriate responsibilities and tasks. This helps build their confidence and fosters a sense of accomplishment. Allow them to handle simple chores or make decisions related to their routine, such as choosing their clothes for the day.

Managing daily routines and interactions involves creating a consistent and predictable environment, using visual aids, easing transitions, and promoting positive interactions. By incorporating these practical tips, you can help your child with PTSD navigate their day with greater ease and confidence.

Chapter 9
Building Resilience and Hope

Fostering resilience and hope in children, especially those dealing with PTSD, is essential for their long-term well-being and emotional growth. Building resilience helps children cope with stress and bounce back from adversity, while instilling hope encourages them to believe in their ability to overcome challenges. Here's how parents can nurture these qualities:

Model Resilience: Children learn a great deal by observing their parents. Show them how to handle setbacks and difficulties with a positive attitude. When faced with challenges, talk openly about your feelings and the steps you're taking to overcome them. Demonstrate problem-solving skills and a determined mindset. For example, if you're dealing with a problem at work, explain the situation to your child in simple terms and describe how you're working through it. This teaches them that problems can be faced and resolved.

Encourage a Growth Mindset: Help your child develop a growth mindset by emphasizing that skills and abilities can be developed with effort and practice. Celebrate their progress, not just the end results. For instance, if your child is struggling with a school subject, praise their hard work and persistence rather than focusing solely on grades. This approach helps them understand that effort leads to improvement and encourages them to keep trying even when things are tough.

Set Realistic Goals: Guide your child in setting and achieving realistic goals. Break down larger tasks into smaller, manageable steps and celebrate each achievement along the way. This builds their confidence and shows them that progress is made through gradual efforts. For example, if your child is working on improving their reading skills, set small, achievable goals like reading a few pages each day and acknowledge their efforts as they reach these milestones.

Teach Problem-Solving Skills: Equip your child with problem-solving skills by involving them in decision-making and brainstorming solutions to problems. Encourage them to think through different options and weigh the pros and cons of each choice. For instance, if your child is facing a conflict with a friend, discuss various ways to address the issue and help them choose the most effective solution. This empowers them to handle challenges independently and confidently.

Promote Positive Self-Talk: Help your child develop a positive inner dialogue by teaching them to replace negative thoughts with constructive ones. Encourage them to use affirmations and positive self-talk when facing difficulties. For example, if your child feels overwhelmed by a task, guide them to say, "I can do this with some effort" rather than focusing on self-doubt. This practice helps them build a resilient mindset and fosters a sense of hope.

Support Emotional Expression: Create a safe space for your child to express their emotions. Validate their feelings and encourage them to talk about their experiences. Use open-ended questions to help them articulate their thoughts and feelings. For instance, you might ask, **"How did that make you feel?"** or **"What can we do to help you feel better?"** This approach helps them process their emotions and reinforces that their feelings are important and manageable.

Celebrate Strengths and Achievements: Regularly acknowledge and celebrate your child's strengths and accomplishments, no matter how small. Highlighting their abilities and achievements helps them build self-esteem and resilience. For example, if your child successfully completes a challenging task, celebrate their effort with positive reinforcement and encouragement. This recognition reinforces their sense of accomplishment and motivates them to tackle future challenges with confidence.

Encourage Healthy Relationships: Foster strong, supportive relationships by encouraging your child to build connections with peers, family members, and mentors. Healthy relationships offer emotional support and a feeling of belonging. Facilitate opportunities for your child to engage in social activities and build friendships. For instance, encourage them to participate in group activities or clubs where they can form meaningful connections with others.

Provide Consistent Support: Be a reliable source of support for your child by offering encouragement and reassurance during difficult times. Let them know that you are always there to help them through challenges and celebrate their successes. Consistent support helps build a strong foundation of trust and security, which is crucial for developing resilience.

Promote Healthy Coping Strategies: Teach your child healthy ways to cope with stress and adversity. Introduce them to relaxation techniques, such as deep breathing or mindfulness, and encourage them to use these strategies when they feel overwhelmed. For example, you might practice deep breathing exercises together during stressful moments and discuss how these techniques can help manage their emotions.

By implementing these techniques, parents can effectively foster resilience and hope in their children, helping them to navigate their challenges with greater confidence and optimism. Building resilience is a process that takes time and patience, but the positive impact on your child's emotional well-being and ability to handle stress will be well worth the effort.

Strategies for maintaining a positive outlook and forward-thinking

Maintaining a positive outlook and a forward-thinking mindset is crucial for both parents and children navigating the challenges of PTSD. A positive attitude helps build resilience, boosts motivation, and promotes overall well-being. Here are strategies for fostering a hopeful and optimistic perspective:

Focus on Strengths and Achievements: Encourage your child to recognize and celebrate their strengths and achievements. Emphasize what they're doing well and how far they've come, rather than dwelling on setbacks. For example, if your child has made progress in their ability to manage anxiety, highlight their improvement and the effort they've put in. This approach shifts focus from problems to accomplishments, fostering a positive self-image and reinforcing their ability to overcome challenges.

Practice Gratitude: Introduce the practice of gratitude to your child by regularly acknowledging things they are thankful for. This can be done through a daily or weekly gratitude journal where they list things they appreciate. Encourage them to reflect on positive experiences and moments of joy. For instance, you might ask your child each evening what they're grateful for, helping them focus on the positive aspects of their life. Practicing gratitude shifts attention from difficulties to the good things in life, fostering a more positive outlook.

Set and Pursue Goals: Help your child set meaningful, achievable goals and support them in working toward these objectives. Divide larger goals into smaller, manageable tasks and celebrate each achievement along the way. This process instills a sense of purpose and direction, keeping them focused on future possibilities. For example, if your child wants to improve their social skills, set specific goals like initiating conversations or joining a new activity, and recognize their progress along the way.

Encourage Problem-Solving and Optimism: Teach your child to approach challenges with a problem-solving mindset. Help them view obstacles as opportunities for growth and learning. When faced with difficulties, guide them to brainstorm potential solutions and discuss how they can tackle issues constructively. For example, if your child struggles with a school project, work together to develop a plan and explore ways to overcome obstacles. This perspective encourages them to see challenges as manageable and solvable, fostering a hopeful outlook.

Model Positive Thinking: Demonstrate a positive attitude in your own life. Children often mirror their parents' attitudes, so showing optimism and resilience in your own challenges can influence their perspective. Share positive affirmations and reinforce the idea that setbacks are temporary and can be overcome. For instance, if you're facing a difficult situation, talk about the positive aspects and the steps you're taking to address it. Your attitude can inspire your child to adopt a similar approach.

Create a Vision Board: Help your child create a vision board with images and words that represent their hopes, dreams, and goals. This visual tool serves as a reminder of their aspirations and encourages a forward-thinking mindset. Spend time together discussing their goals and the steps needed to achieve them. For example, if your child dreams of becoming an artist, include pictures of art supplies, inspiring artists, and their own artwork on the board. This practice keeps their focus on positive possibilities and motivates them to pursue their dreams.

Encourage Positive Self-Talk: Help your child substitute negative thoughts with positive affirmations. Help them identify and challenge negative self-talk, and encourage them to use affirmations that promote self-belief and optimism. For example, if your child thinks, "**I can't do this**," guide them to reframe it as, "**I can try my best and improve with practice**." Positive self-talk reinforces a hopeful mindset and boosts confidence.

Promote Healthy Routines: Establishing and maintaining healthy routines can contribute to a positive outlook. Encourage your child to engage in activities that promote well-being, such as regular exercise, balanced nutrition, and adequate sleep. Consistent routines provide a sense of stability and contribute to emotional resilience. For instance, incorporate regular physical activity into your child's daily schedule, and discuss how it helps them feel better and manage stress.

Celebrate Small Wins: Acknowledge and celebrate small victories and progress. Recognizing even minor achievements boosts motivation and reinforces a positive perspective. For example, if your child successfully completes a challenging task or overcomes a fear, celebrate their accomplishment with praise or a small reward. This practice helps them focus on their successes and fosters a sense of accomplishment.

Encourage Social Connections: Support your child in building and maintaining positive relationships with friends and family. Social connections provide emotional support and contribute to a positive outlook. Encourage them to spend time with people who uplift and inspire them. For example, facilitate playdates or family gatherings where your child can connect with others and enjoy positive interactions. Strong social ties contribute to a hopeful and optimistic perspective.

By implementing these strategies, parents can help their children maintain a positive outlook and foster a forward-thinking mindset. A hopeful perspective not only supports emotional resilience but also empowers children to face challenges with confidence and optimism.

Conclusion
Recap of main strategies and support provided

In parenting a child with PTSD, you have embarked on a challenging yet profoundly impactful journey. This book has provided a range of strategies and insights to support you in nurturing your child through trauma. As we bring our discussion to a close, let's revisit the main strategies and support that can help you along this path.

Creating a Safe Environment: One of the foundational elements in supporting your child is establishing a trauma-informed environment. This involves creating a space where your child feels physically and emotionally safe. Consistency, routines, and stability are key here. A predictable routine helps your child feel secure, reducing anxiety and fostering a sense of normalcy. Remember to create both physical and emotional safety by offering reassurance, maintaining open lines of communication, and being a steady presence in your child's life.

Supporting Emotional Regulation: Helping your child manage their emotions effectively is crucial. Techniques such as mindfulness practices and relaxation exercises can be valuable tools. Encouraging activities that promote calmness and emotional balance, like deep breathing or guided imagery, helps your child handle stress more effectively. Additionally, teaching them how to cope with anxiety and stress through practical strategies can empower them to manage their feelings in a healthy way.

Working with Professionals: Navigating the professional support system is an important aspect of managing PTSD. Finding the right therapist or counselor is crucial. Understand the different types of therapy available, such as cognitive-behavioral therapy or play therapy, and choose one that best fits your child's needs. Effective collaboration with mental health professionals involves clear communication and setting mutual goals. Monitoring and understanding therapy progress ensures that the support your child receives is aligned with their needs.

Self-Care for Parents: Taking care of your own well-being is equally important. Managing stress and maintaining emotional health as a parent helps you stay resilient and better support your child. Setting boundaries, finding balance, and establishing self-care routines are essential strategies. Remember to seek support and build a network of people who can offer encouragement and assistance. Resources like counseling and support groups can provide valuable support for your own mental health.

Practical Strategies for Everyday Challenges: Addressing specific issues such as nightmares, flashbacks, and anxiety requires practical strategies. Developing approaches for handling school and social situations, balancing discipline with support, and managing daily routines helps create a stable and supportive environment for your child. These strategies ensure that you are equipped to deal with the everyday challenges that arise in the context of PTSD.

Building Resilience and Hope: Fostering resilience and hope in your child is a vital aspect of their recovery journey. Techniques for encouraging a positive outlook, setting goals, and celebrating achievements build a sense of hope and optimism. Maintaining a positive perspective and encouraging forward-thinking helps your child remain motivated and resilient in the face of challenges.

Throughout this book, you've been equipped with a range of strategies to support your child effectively. Your role as a parent is crucial in providing the love, stability, and guidance they need. By implementing these strategies and maintaining a focus on your child's well-being, you contribute significantly to their healing and growth. Remember, every step you take in supporting your child is a step towards a brighter, more hopeful future for both you and them.

Final words of encouragement and motivation

As we close this chapter, I want to reach out to you with all the warmth and compassion of a fellow parent who understands the depths of your journey. Parenting a child with PTSD is a path filled with both challenges and triumphs. You have shown incredible strength, love, and resilience in navigating this journey, and it's important to acknowledge the enormous effort you're making every day.

Remember, every small step you take, every moment of patience, and every act of kindness you show your child is a testament to your unwavering commitment and love. Your presence in their life is a beacon of hope and stability, guiding them through their struggles and helping them find their way to a brighter future.

I know there will be days when the path feels particularly steep, when the emotional weight seems heavy, and when doubt tries to creep in. But in those moments, remember that you are not alone. Your dedication is powerful, and the love you give is a force that nurtures and heals. Embrace the highs and lows, and trust that your efforts are making a profound difference.

You have the strength to weather the storms and the courage to face the challenges head-on. Celebrate the victories, no matter how small they may seem, and be gentle with yourself on the tough days. Your role as a parent is not just about guiding your child but also about taking care of your own heart and soul. In the quiet moments of reflection, hold on to the hope and love that brought you to this point. Your journey is one of immense courage and compassion, and it's shaping a future where your child can thrive despite the challenges they face. Keep moving forward with the knowledge that you are doing everything in your power to create a safe, nurturing, and hopeful environment for them.

You are doing an extraordinary job. Trust in your strength, lean on your support network, and keep believing in the power of love and resilience. Your child's journey is unique, and so is yours as a parent. Together, you're navigating this path with grace, and every step you take is paving the way for a brighter tomorrow.

© Clara Jennings